HOW TO L[...]
WINNING G[...]

by

David M. Barber

**I dedicate the Network Marketing Academy and The STARS
Leadership Programme
to those distributors, dream-creators,
with the wisdom to learn,
who care enough about their people's success to want to show
them the way,
and with the *Focus* and *Bulldozer Mentality* to bring their
ATAC Lifeplan to life.**

> If you want to see how David Barber can help you explode your
> business, turn to
> **www.davidbarberinternational.com**

The Network Marketing Academy

First published by Insight Publishing Limited in 1996
Second edition published by Cedar Publishing Limited in
April 2003
This third edition published by The Network Marketing
Academy in October 2003.

Cover illustration by Jonathan Goulding Illustration & Design

Published by The Network Marketing Academy Limited
7, Braddons Cliffe
Braddons Hill Road East
Torquay
Devon TQ1 1HR.
Phone/fax 01803 296733

ISBN 1-899298-05-3

Acknowledgements

I am indebted to Peter Bloomfield for his kind permission to use his
telephoning system, a most important contribution to business
building. The Business Activity Agreement (BACTA) was
developed from an idea originally discussed with Martin Kern.

Notice of Liability

Printed and bound in Great Britain by Bath Press Limited, Bath.

≈CONTENTS≈

≈INTRODUCTION≈

One of the most exciting things in life is to watch people, under your care and guidance and through a series of simple steps, create sometimes awesome outcomes. That is what winning *teachers* do. One of the most exciting gifts you can give anyone is the opportunity to make something of their own lives: to give them the vehicle, by your inspiration show them how to use it and then take them to heights of which they had previously only dreamt. That is what winning *leaders* do.

This book covers the training and leadership aspects of **The STARS Leadership Programme,** the advanced series of The Network Marketing Academy, the first and so far only fully comprehensive home-learning and tuition programme available to the network marketing industry. The STARS Leadership Programme follows on from *The Secrets Series*, and consists of five books:

- Get Off To A Winning Start In Network Marketing
- Breakthrough Recruiting & Retailing
- How To Lead A Winning Group (this book)
- Target Success!
- Network Marketeers… Supercharge Yourself!

Planning for Success is an essential skill for you to both practise and teach. To get your people into this with the minimum of effort on your part, introduce them to *Target Success!* This valuable aid includes all the forms they will need for planning during the whole of their first year (including everything they need for their Contact List), and it also offers an easy way to deal with uninspiring but essential topics such as how to do their accounts and VAT returns.

Network Marketeers… Supercharge Yourself! introduces you to the fascinating field of **Personal Development,** the science of developing the right **Attitudes** for success, one of the Eight Must-do Activities and absolutely essential to being a winning teacher and leader— so essential that most big business builders consider it even more important than learning about the business.

STARS stands for seven of the Eight Must-do Activities:

The Eight Must-do Activities
Support Events **T**each and **T**arget **A**ttitudes **R**ecruit and **R**etail **S**tructure Your Group

The eighth Must-do Activity, **Leadership,** is in the title of the Programme itself.

We have already covered all the basic knowledge, techniques and attitudes which you need to be a successful distributor in *The Secrets Series* and in the two earlier titles in the STARS Leadership Programme: *Get Off To A Winning Start In Network Marketing* and *Breakthrough Recruiting & Retailing.* The purpose of this book is to show you how to pass that information on to your people in the best possible way. It is *not* to teach you that information. So, if you have not been through all those previous titles can I suggest that you do so before going any further. The terms that were introduced earlier in *The Secrets Series* and the Programme are covered in a Glossary at the back of the book.

~ ~ ~

Many people want to be leaders. One reason why few succeed is because, although the desire is there, they do not know how to and there is no one to show them. *If you are worried that you do not have the makings of leadership within you, or that you have no previous experience of teaching or leadership—don't be!*

Anyone can be a winning teacher and leader

One of the maxims of The STARS Leadership Programme is that everything can be put into practice by *The least experienced, least confident, least talented slowest learners*, and this is as true of this book as of everything else. No matter how little natural ability, management or business experience you have, at the completion of our journey together you will have all the knowledge you need to become a winning leader and teacher, whether you want to build a small but profitable group, or join those elite few who have reached the dizzy heights at the top of a profession where incomes are measured in six figures a *month*.

"Give me your determination, give me your action, give me your willingness to learn, and I will show you the way"

That is my commitment to you. The only proviso is that your actions are **Rocket Actions, not Catherine wheel Actions.** A Catherine wheel may look and sound terrific as it *whooshes*, spins and showers sparks in all directions, but it is going nowhere! Despite all its power, it can never hit its target so all its actions are in vain. Instead, it needs to emulate a rocket, aimed unerringly at its target. The majority of distributors waste their energies in Catherine wheel actions. They can work as hard as they like, but it doesn't matter because they're going nowhere. Before they can succeed, they, too, need to emulate a rocket, aimed unerringly at their purposes.

By the end of this Programme, you will be able to make the same commitment to the people you teach and to the group you lead, even if you are right now one of *The least experienced, least confident, least talented slowest learners*.

~ ~ ~

A massive shortage of leaders and teachers—a major industry problem

In conventional business, promotion is hard to come by: getting one promotion in two years is exceptional. Reaching the top of a corporate tree usually takes decades, if ever! Although exceptional talents can be held back by this system, people are given the time to grow gradually into the skills of teaching and leadership.

One of the great attractions of network marketing is that you are "promoted" as fast as you can "make it". In the hothouse atmosphere of network marketing, distributors become instant teachers and leaders the minute they recruit their first person; in their first year they can have maybe six "promotions" and may even reach the top of the "corporate" tree.

The downside is that this creates huge numbers of inexperienced leaders and teachers. Add to this that the majority of distributors have never had any previous management experience and that such training schemes as exist for teaching and leadership are sadly deficient, and it is easy to see why the vast majority of distributors struggle when it comes to leading and teaching their groups. All group building is seriously held back because of this.

Fast promotion also breeds the belief that, because a distributor has built a business and can motivate groups of people, they must be a good leader and teacher. That does not necessarily follow. It may well be that they have achieved this though personal charisma, and luck can also play a big part. Neither of these is duplicatable. The danger is to believe that because charismatic people can and do get there without conventional training, everyone else can do the same. That is a complete fallacy, as our interview with Motivator Michael (Chapter 3) illustrates very well.

The industry has never come to terms with how to teach people to become good teachers and leaders *overnight*. However, this is not an insuperable problem, and finding a solution was my vision behind creating The STARS Leadership Programme, which for the first time shows how you can create many more downline leaders and trainers and make them much more effective.

Just as in the worlds of sport and conventional business, there is a wealth of people in network marketing who have the potential to reach the top level, *provided they are given the right training and support*. In every group the potential is there *right now* to make existing leaders better and to blossom budding leaders into flower.

Feed yourself in Bite-Size Chunks!

There is a great deal of valuable detail in this book, but don't blow yourself out of the Programme by trying to assimilate it too quickly. Take your time. You are better off spending a week on one chapter and applying it properly than in rushing through the book and overwhelming yourself. In the first case, you will become a winning teacher and leader; in the second, you will not.

~ ~ ~

PART I

Teaching And Leadership: What Do They Mean In Network Marketing?

Because we are talking about teachers and leaders, there is a danger that people will read this as suggesting that teachers and leaders are different to distributors. They are not.

Where teaching is concerned, all distributors are teachers

Teaching is one of the Eight Must-do Activities. Through the culture of **Making sure that people are accompanied in everything they do,** *a maxim of The STARS Leadership Programme is:*

Teaching the job *is* doing it, and doing the job *is* teaching it

---

So when we talk about teachers, we mean one aspect of a distributor's job, which is teaching.

Every distributor with at least one person in their group is also a leader, but it is your choice whether you choose a high-level (what we call active) or low-level role.

≈CHAPTER 1≈

"Do I Have What It Takes To Be A Leader And Teacher?"

Before we discuss whether you have what it takes to be a leader and teacher, let's answer this question:

"Do I *have* to be a leader and teacher?"

If you only need a small group to earn the income you want, you can delegate your teaching and leadership roles upline and let them do it all for you. You only need to get involved if you cannot find uplines to delegate to. Then of course you have a responsibility to support your people properly.

If you want a medium sized group, you will need to take an active teaching role in terms of making sure your people are accompanied in everything they do. With regard to leadership, you need do no more than plug your group into the uplines who have taken on the active classroom trainings and leadership roles of the group to which you belong (**The Figure-of-Eight Attitude,** Chapter 7, *Get Off To A Winning Start*).

If you are looking for a serious income, you will need to become an active leader. But this does not mean you have to lay on BOMs, trainings and events, unless, of course, they do not exist in the areas where your group needs them. Nor do you need to become a public speaker—although it will help your cause if you do.

Whatever sized group you want, you must still give your people a good example by encouraging them to follow the On-Track Path, go to meetings and trainings, and support your uplines' efforts to create a strong, successful group. And you have a duty to help any downline distributor if there is no one else on hand to help them.

If you are one of the very rare breed of charismatic leaders, every-one will benefit if you use your recruiting talents to concentrate on the high profile roles (these will become obvious later) and leave your distributors free to devote their time to teaching the group.

"What talent do I need?"

Let's get two things into perspective:

First, success as a leader and teacher only means knowing what to say when, and knowing what to do when, with the right attitudes. Second:

Being a winning teacher or leader does not mean having to be better at the job than anyone else!

Many people think they are not good enough at the job to teach or lead. However, being no great shakes at retailing and recruiting is no barrier to becoming a very big business-builder. I have been privileged to sit in on Get-Active phone calls and 2-2-2s with some of the great business-builders. Some, yes, are real artists on the phone and at recruiting and retailing. But most of them really are no better than "OK", yet they have big businesses. You see, they understand the Keystone Law: *Your path to success lies ONLY through the success of your people.* They know that getting the best out of other people is much more important than how good or bad they themselves happen to be. In fact:

Being good at a job can actually be a disadvantage! Some of the best recruiters and retailers make the worst leaders and teachers

---

A person who knows that they are good very often spends too much time doing the job instead of teaching other people to do it. Many teachers also insist on taking over a job (and how infuriating they are!) instead of letting their people get on with it, on the grounds that their people cannot do it as well as they can.

Being good at a job can also lead to impatience with others who are not as good at it as you are, and that is bad teaching and leadership.

There is a lot in common between being a good network marketing teacher and a good sports coach; Coach Charles is a top sports coach and we will be talking to him later. He isn't very good at his sport, yet he is reckoned to be one of the best people around at helping other people to excel in that field. In fact, almost no coach in the world is as good at their sport as their top athletes. Many are not even as good at the sport as their *worst*! If you think about it, the job of a sports coach is to show people how to do the job better than the coach can do it—in fact, vastly better than they can.

Your job as a winning teacher is not to do the job well yourself, it is to help other people to be as good as *they* can, or want to, be.

Your job as a winning teacher is to be the best you can be at *teaching* it, not at *doing* it

---

Remember, too, that network marketing is peculiar in that, as I said before, doing the job *is* teaching it and teaching the job *is* doing it.

I said it in both previous titles of the Programme but it bears repeating: there is nothing difficult about teaching or leading. The whole nub is that if people trust you *enough*, like you *enough* and respect you *enough* (and "enough" is the key word here), they will learn anything from you and will follow your leadership. These are all qualities that anyone can develop. You will see nothing there about having to be good at your job, articulate, attractive, intelligent, charismatic or well-educated. Although all these will help if you are trusted, liked and respected, *none of them will make up for a lack of those qualities*.

Anyone who can fight for what they believe in can be a leader

Do you doubt that, if your child was lost and there were no emergency services available to mount a search, you could mobilise friends, neighbours and passers-by into action, and into Rocket Action at that? If you can be a leader under those circumstances, you can be a leader under *any* circumstances. You just need to feel strongly enough about your success.

I apologise to dustmen and farm labourers when I ask this question, but would you class them as natural leaders? Yet, when Christ picked His apostles to create one of the biggest organisations human society has ever known, He did not chose natural leaders but, in today's terms, dustmen and farm labourers. In their lifetimes, these people, most of whom could not read or write, created international "groups" using what would now be called network marketing techniques, including what we now call BOMs and sizzle sessions. If they could do that and without the use of cars, trains, phones, faxes, the internet, emails or websites, or overnight mail, every one of you can build the far smaller group you will need to create the income you want. It all depends on whether your purpose is strong enough.

Leaders can be made, not born

In the early days of soccer there was little priority put on training, so the most talented players automatically rose to the top. The trouble was that there were nowhere near enough talented players to go around. Then clubs discovered that they could make a bunch of less talented *trained* players beat a team of more talented *untrained* players. Now, in every professional sport, a coach who is after a winner will every time pick a less talented sportsperson who learns hard and trains hard over a more talented person who does not.

In business, too, it is very well proven that a less talented *trained* manager will go further than a more talented *untrained* manager.

If you do not consider yourself to be a born teacher and leader but are prepared to pay the price of making yourself one by putting into practice what I show you, and if you surround yourself with like-minded people, you can feel confident that you will build a vastly bigger business than those greatly talented leaders who build their hopes on the few untrained but talented "natural leaders" who happen to land in their group.

~ ~ ~

≈CHAPTER 2≈

The On-Track Path: Reviewing The Basics

Before moving onto new ground, I would like to remind you of some of the points we have covered in The STARS Leadership Programme and *The Secrets Series*.

The Eight Must-do Activities

Everything in network marketing, and therefore your teaching and leadership, must revolve around these.

The Six Winning Attitudes

The Six Winning Attitudes are the Must-do Activity that drive the other seven. They determine *exactly* how well you will recruit, retail, lead, teach, target, support events and structure your group, and *exactly* how successful your business will be. So it is worth pulling them together for you:

- **Have Pride.** Have pride in:
  - ✓ Your opportunity and your product
  - ✓ The industry of network marketing
  - ✓ Yourself
  - ✓ Your group.
- **Have Focus.** The points of Focus are:
  - ✓ Recruit...... Recruit...... Recruit......
  - ✓ Retailing is the life-blood of the business
  - ✓ This is a teaching business
  - ✓ EVERY distributor is a leader
  - ✓ No one ever succeeded by not supporting meetings and events
  - ✓ Build deep, as well as wide
  - ✓ Focus on your purposes

- ✓ Focus your actions on your purposes by planning, to create Rocket Action.
- **Have A Bulldozer Mentality** so that you can plough through every obstacle.
- **Be Patient** in the following ways:
  - ✓ Give the Geometric Progression time to work
  - ✓ When recruiting or teaching, Unfold At Their Speed, not yours
  - ✓ Give yourself the time to learn properly (give yourself a six months' apprenticeship)
  - ✓ Anchor legs properly before you leave them (I will cover this later).
- **Be Hungry To Learn:**
  - ✓ Use the Learning LAWR (Chapter 7, *Get Off To A Winning Start*). Build a library of books, tapes, CDs and videos on your opportunity, network marketing and personal development, and develop the Thirty-Minutes-A-Day Habit
  - ✓ Treat every situation as a learning situation.
- **People Buy People.** So "sell yourself" to the three groups of people who make up your business:
  - ✓ Potential distributors
  - ✓ Distributors already in your business
  - ✓ Customers for the product.

In carrying out your job as a leader and teacher, I want to highlight two of the Six Winning Attitudes are of outstanding importance to your success. These are having Focus and a Bulldozer Mentality.

Focus and a Bulldozer Mentality

We are particularly interested in two areas of Focus: *Focus on your purposes* and *Focus your actions on success by planning*. These create the Rocket Actions which, together with your Bulldozer Mentality, will keep you going until you get to where you want, especially if you want to get there as fast as you can.

But, more important, they create momentum and your first job is to get momentum into your group. This does not mean that you need to be full-time but it does mean that you must accept that *you* are the **Momentum Generator,** the Driver, behind your group.

There are only two sources of momentum: your *Focus* and your *Bulldozer Mentality*

If you think about it, one way to phrase the purpose of this book is: *To make the results of your Momentum Generation, your Driving Force, as productive as possible.*

There are two basic ground rules to teaching and leadership:

1. **The results must always be more important than the technique. The only purpose of teaching and leadership is to get better results**

2. *No amount of knowledge will make up for any loss of Focus or a Bulldozer Mentality.* **If by learning you lose even 1% of your Focus or Bulldozer Mentality, stop learning and start acting!**

I want to put teaching and leadership into perspective. Many top earners have become so purely with Focus and a Bulldozer Mentality, acquiring little knowledge of how to help others to succeed (Motivator Michael, Chapter 3). They may not have done much of a job for most of their people, but it shows that Focus and a Bulldozer Mentality are a great deal more important than knowledge.

But I challenge you to find the reverse: a distributor who lacked Focus and a Bulldozer Mentality, yet became a high earner on the strength of their knowledge.

The Keystone Law

The Six Winning Attitudes are themselves inspired by the **Keystone Law**—which, of course, means that the better you teach and lead your people, the more successful you will be.

The Theory of Duplication

The Theory of Duplication is the basis of all successful teaching, and was covered in Chapter 16 of *Get Off To A Winning Start*.

The On-Track Path

Being on track means:

- Putting in the time and the effort they promised *and*
- Willing to learn from you and to let you accompany them in everything they do *and*
- Willing to *apply* what they learn with the right attitudes, particularly having Focus and a Bulldozer Mentality.

To remind you that it takes all three elements to be on the On-Track Path; if only one is missing, that person is already off track.

Avoid situations of Dependency

Dependency means one of two things:

- That a distributor has learnt to depend on you to build their business for them
- That they are only prepared to work only when you are actually *with* them.

The first is the result of bad tuition. It means that, often due to impatience, while you are actually with a distributor you take over jobs which they are capable of doing for themselves, and this develops into a habit of letting you do the work. To avoid this, ensure that you make a distributor do all the jobs their current expertise allows them to, until the point comes when they are doing all the work and you are simply there to advise.

The second situation means that the distributor lacks motivation. Unless something is found to motivate them, they will drop out. They are already off track and, as a result, you should not be working with them anyway except to help them to recruit some of their own contacts before they drop out. Of course, by doing this you might turn them into active distributors.

~ ~ ~

≈CHAPTER 3≈

The Differences Between Leadership, Motivation And Training

People get confused over the differences between leadership, motivation and training, and the three words are, as a result, often used interchangeably. The correct relationship is:

Winning Leadership =
MOTIVATION + TRAINING + Direction

So motivation and training are distinct parts of leadership and require different skills. Let's now see how the three differ (I will come back to direction later in the book).

1. How leading and teaching differ

A leader lays down the path the group must follow, whereas a teacher works individually with people showing them in detail how to follow that path. Some people are good leaders, others are good teachers but few are naturally good at both. I will show you how to overcome that.

2. How leadership and motivation differ

Motivation is thriving in network marketing. The industry gives room to charisma to blossom, and most networks and large groups boast strong, compelling leaders and speakers, exercising powerful motivational forces on their businesses. Motivator Michael is one such person. In fact, he calls network marketing, "the ultimate motivational business". I asked him how he saw his role as a leader.

'That's easy,' he said. 'This is a very simple business. All it takes is the *right attitude* and *anyone* can succeed in it. My job as a leader is to point out to everyone what the opportunities are, show them what the right attitude is—and then motivate them to keep going!'

'What do you define as the right attitude?' I asked.

'First, have what I call a ***Bulldozer Mentality***—in other words, just keep going whatever the obstacles are
↓

'Then ***be teachable.*** Just do what I and the other front-runners do, and you will be all right
↓

'Then ***be credible.*** Your prospects have got to ***believe*** what you say—if they don't, you'll never sign anybody up!
↓

'Then put in ***massive action***! If you don't Do, you won't Get
↓

'After that, all you need to do is: ***teach other people to do the same.***'

'Is that all?' I asked.

'Yes, this business is incredibly simple. Just get a Contact List together→then show the product→show the business→invite your prospect to a BOM [not all companies promote BOMs]→sign them up→then tell them to do exactly what you've just done...... and Bob's your Uncle—you're on your way to a fortune! Provided that people put in massive action and stick to recruiting, retailing and teaching, that's it—they can't go wrong!'

'But they do go wrong, don't they!' I exclaimed.

'Yes,' Motivator Michael said. 'And I just cannot understand why! Do you know, this is the easiest business I have ever been in? Surely it can't be harder than what they were doing before and I know that, whatever else most of them do, it can't offer anything like the income, the freedom and the enjoyment that this business can. So just why don't they make it?'

Motivator Michael belongs to a group of people for whom network marketing might have been tailor-made, those with what can variously be described as having **charisma, magnetic personalities** or **natural leadership qualities.** They can find it relatively plain sailing because what sets them apart is a God-given gift to simply carry people along with them.

Motivator Michael tells everyone that his Bulldozer Mentality got him to the top and, if people will copy what he did (which is what he means by being teachable), they, too, can get to the top. But he has got his equation wrong: he has left out his magic ingredient of charisma. I have seen many distributors try to copy the great motivational network marketeers and come badly unstuck because they can duplicate their Bulldozer Mentality, they can duplicate their sense of *Urgency in Action*, they can become equally focused, but no one can duplicate their charisma. They either have it or they haven't.

That does not mean that you cannot build a major network without charisma—you most definitely can! But it does mean that:

> **Those of us who lack charisma have no choice but to base our success on providing professional teaching and leadership.**

3. How motivation and training differ

- **Motivation** is what makes people take action
- **Training** is teaching people what to do when they take action.

People who confuse motivation with training think that, once they have motivated someone to act, they have also taught them *how* to act. Because of this confusion, many initial trainings are in fact more motivation than training. The result is that new distributors leave all fired up ready to go, only to be brought up short when they think: *"But what do I do now?"*

'I'm greatly motivated—but what am I supposed to *do?*'

Motivation without training is largely wasted because the only people able to benefit will be those who *already* know what to do.

Most of the training in our industry only teaches the people to succeed who would have succeeded anyway

That to my mind is not successful leadership. That is providing *anyone* who wants to succeed with the knowledge and support (Motivation + Training + Direction) to make it.

The purpose of The STARS Leadership Programme is to give you the tools to help the people to succeed who would not have succeeded without you

Who are the people to whom you have to give knowledge and support? Distributors, of course. But that covers a very diverse range of people, so let's have a closer look at them now.

~ ~ ~

≈CHAPTER 4≈

Your ONLY Path To Success—Your People's Success

This is the Keystone Law, and there is only one way to turn it to your advantage: through leadership and teaching. They are the powers given to you to unlock the success of your distributors in order to create your own success.

What makes people dream-creators?

In network marketing, just as in every field of human endeavour:

It is the right *Knowledge* and *Attitudes* that turn people's *Actions* into success

---

Action is the key here because, without it, nothing happens: there *is* no success. So whatever other purposes your leadership and teaching have, they must result in people taking not just action, but Rocket Action.

As a teacher and leader, the secret to making people take action is simple:

When someone sees an action as a "must", they will do it. When they see a desired result as a "must", they will go for it

---

The hard part, of course, is to get people to accept actions, especially Rocket Actions, as "musts". But the more successfully you can do that, the more successful you will be.

However, how *much* action people take, how *determined* they are in their actions and how *successful* those actions are all depend on their **attitudes.** Where **knowledge** fits in is:

**If *Attitudes* decide how well your people *will* act,
Knowledge decides how well they *can* act**

Therefore, giving them knowledge that does not result in more Rocket Action, more determined Rocket Action or better Rocket Action, is wasted.

So, as well as the purpose of leadership and teaching being to unlock the power of the Keystone Law, we can say that:

The purpose of leadership and teaching is to create in your people the *Attitudes* and *Rocket Actions* they need for success, and to give them the *Knowledge* to do that as well as possible.

Who are the people you will teach or lead?

Your distributors will fall into five categories:

1. Distributors who want to be led

Although this sounds contrary to the concept of network marketing, in which the appeal is supposed to be that everyone is their own boss, *the majority of distributors by far come into this category.* Rather than wanting to "run their own businesses", most of them would rather be treated as "employed" in the sense that they are happier following instructions than giving them, and they are more comfortable having someone else make the decisions for them. They are happier being part of a group in which they can see a hierarchy of strong leadership. Well, if that is what these distributors want from you as their leader then that is what you must give them.

Having said that, if these distributors want to succeed, *they must still accept the responsibilities of leading their own group.* However, although essential, the leadership they must display is of a very easy and low level (Chapter 9 under the heading *How To Teach Distributors To Lead Their Group*).

2. The "top dogs"

These are people who like to exercise as much control over their group as they can, if possible setting up their own trainings, BOMs and other events, and even controlling the flow of recruitment and training materials into their group. Just as few people want to be the chief executive of a major corporation, so there will be only a tiny percentage of the total network who aspire to be "top dogs".

"Top dogs" are not necessarily cross-line of each other; one "top dog" may be downline of another. Unlike top managers in conventional business, who see other aspiring "top dogs" as a threat to their own position and therefore try to stifle them, everyone in network marketing is panting to attract such people because these are the people who will boost them to wealth! Indeed, the perfect position is to find and develop "top dog" distributors in *every* leg of your business because you would now be earning a fortune for doing absolutely nothing apart, possibly, from having to qualify!

3. First lieutenants

These are distributors who, although they want to be recognised as leaders, do not want to be "top dogs". Some distributors in this category will have small groups, others will have very large ones— in fact, the largest of them may well have around 50% or more of a "top dog's" business. Therefore, they qualify in their own right as big business-builders.

Like those in the first category, first lieutenants like to work in a structure. But unlike those in the first category, they want to be part of the group's decision-making process—they want to run their own group but entirely within the umbrella of a "top dog's" group. In conventional business, they would be on the board of directors, but would not want to be managing director or chairman.

Some first lieutenants may be on their way to splitting off their group to become "top dogs" in their own right. (Don't confuse this with what is called a **Breakaway Group.** In many compensation plans, once a distributor reaches a certain position on the plan, their group *automatically* "breaks away" from their upline businesses. But this does not mean they want to sever connections with the main group unless they intend to be "top dogs" in their own right)

4. The talkers, not the doers

These are the sheep in wolves' clothing and, until you learn to recognise them, can waste a lot of your time because they pay lip-service to the On-Track Path but don't actually follow it.

Having said that, although they are dream-dumpers, they can be very supportive of you, attending meetings, turning out to events and agreeing with everything the speakers say, even if they do not do it themselves. They will also often help you, if asked. To some of them, network marketing is more like a social life that earns them a little money. Others would like to be successful but never seem to get down to actually doing it; they usually drop out.

See if you can spot Jeremiah the Learning Junky because he is a very common dream-dumper in network marketing; you bump into him at meetings. Jeremiah knows a lot about the business. In fact, you are so impressed by his knowledge of it that you decide to find out more. Your conversation will go something like this:

> *'You obviously know a lot about network marketing.*
> *How long have you been in it?'*
> *'About six months now.'*
> *'Really? How big is your business?'*
> *'Well, I haven't actually **started** yet! I'm just getting*
> *all my facts right first.'*

Sorry, Jeremiah, but the only way to really to learn is to do the job! And, much as you know about the theory, you haven't learnt the effect of the Theory of Duplication—if you spend weeks or months learning about the business before you actually contact anyone, *so will your people!* Which means not a lot of recruiting going on.

Norman the Network Marketing Junky, another dream-dumper, also comes into this category and he is often not supportive of you. He has been in every network invented, sometimes several at once, but failed in all of them. He, too, knows it all but, to cover his failure, he may use that to try to show your people how little *you* know and everything that is wrong with your product, your company, your compensation plan and your trainings. Because he talks with authority (and he may well have more experience in the industry than you), he can dent the confidence of new distributors. Fortunately, it is usually not long before he moves on to irritate another network.

5. The "lone wolves"

These distributors are determined to be in sole charge of their group, so they discourage upline contact with their people. They are active, positive leaders, often highly motivated, hard working and committed to their dream, but they rarely succeed because they insist on going their own way. These are some of the people who drown in the marsh on their way to the City of Dreams (Chapter 6, *Get Off To A Winning Start*), rather than turn back and ask you the way.

This makes them major contributors to the drop-out rate because, when they fall out of the business, they leave a leaderless team who then also drop out.

I find this the saddest group of all because they work really hard to dream-create and they deserve better reward for their efforts. But if someone does not want to be teachable you cannot make them so.

Where do you fit into the team?

Leaving aside the "lone wolves", you can see that every group organises itself into a leadership hierarchy, just like a traditional business. *Indeed, it is important that this is so because without it the* T*eamwork (part of the Leaders' ACTTER, see later), which is so important to success, would be impossible.* You cannot have teamwork without structure in your business.

This means that, although people are free to run their businesses in any way they want, it really is only the freedom to choose how they want to be part of the structure and the team and increase their chances of dream-creating, or, just like the "lone wolves", not be part of the set up and almost certainly become dream-dumpers.

In which category do you see yourself?

Now you have a better picture of the role you are taking on, it is important that you understand the pitfalls involved. Just as every new distributor needs to be warned about *The Pigs Around The Corner*, you are more likely to succeed if you know what difficulties to expect as a teacher and leader. So, before we go any further, let's warn you about the *Pigs* that may be lurking around *your* corner!

~ ~ ~

≈CHAPTER 5≈

The "Pigs Around The Corner" For Leaders And Teachers

We covered *The Pigs Around The Corner* for new distributors in Chapter 5 of *Get Off To A Winning Start*. The "Pigs" I cover here are those which affect you as a leader and teacher:

1. Getting people to make Get-Active phone calls
2. People not being teachable
3. The potential for fast promotion
4. Sponsors not accepting reSPONSORbility
5. Human nature
6. The need to attract leaders
7. Giving your leaders the wrong type of support.

1. Getting enough Get-Active phone calls is *A Pig*

One of your hardest jobs as a teacher and leader is to get your people to make enough Get-Active phone calls. This is somewhat unfortunate when it turns out to be the single most important activity in network marketing, because if not enough recruiting is going on for whatever reason, it boils down to not a lack of Get-Active calls.

There is a mass of detail to winning teaching and leading, but none of it is of much use if you or your group are not making enough calls. The whole STARS Leadership Programme needs to be looked at with that in mind.

The more successful you are at getting your people to make Get-Active phone calls, the more successful you will be as a teacher and leader.

---

2. People not being teachable is *A Pig*

The industry is hoist on its own petard. We constantly preach: *it is a simple business—anyone and everyone can do it*. This leads people to the apparently obvious, but incorrect, conclusion that there is not much to learn, so much so that the majority put no priority on learning at all. *If it is so simple,* they think, *why bother?*

When we say *simple*, we mean that anyone can learn what has to be learnt, we do not mean that there is nothing to learn. It also does not mean that you can do anything you like and still succeed in building a business; in fact, the business becomes devilishly difficult for anyone who is off track.

The fact is that the business is only simple at its lowest levels. The maxim, so prevalent in the industry, *Show the business, show the product and show others how to do the same* may work well enough for small business-builders, but it should be evident that one cannot build and control a business of any size without taking teaching and leadership seriously—especially if one wants a group of several thousand distributors turning over millions of pounds. The leadership skills required may be very much easier to learn than those needed in traditional business, but, unless they are one of a tiny percentage of natural charismatic leaders, anyone wanting to build a full-time business is going to have to learn a few skills.

The problem, as was said in The City of Dreams story (Chapter 6, *Get Off To A Winning Start*) is that:

If people *know* they don't know, you can teach them. if people *think* they know, you can't

---

That points to the first job you as a teacher have: to make sure the distributor you are about to work with knows that they do not know, because if they think they know, you won't be able to teach them anything, and you might as well pack up and go home.

One solution is to tell people *before* they sign up that:
- There is a learning process to go through
- They are going to have to invest in training
- They are going to have to go through a learning curve.

3. The potential for fast promotion is *A Pig*

We looked at this in the Introduction.

4. Sponsors not accepting reSPONSORbility

These of course are simply recruiters—sign people in and then let them get on with it. The problem is not confined to sponsors: many uplines also refuse to accept responsibility for their downlines.

I am not arguing the morality of this; I am only concerned about the problem it causes you as a leader. It may seem obvious to you that, if someone asks a prospect to join their business, they immediately accept a re*sponsor*bility to help that person succeed, but many of your people will not see it that way.

Unfortunately, a tiny proportion of people in every network, those with charisma, hit the top position in the compensation plan with this attitude. Motivator Michael in Chapter 3 exists in every mature network. This makes the problem worse when you are trying to promote good training, as they create a misleading impression that it is possible to reach the top with a "sink or swim" mentality towards distributors. What they do not tell you is that if they had supported their people more creatively:

1. They would have reached where they are now a great deal quicker and more easily
2. Their groups would have been even bigger
3. Unless you have charisma, you haven't a hope of copying them.

The fact is that the average distributor is simply shooting themselves in the foot unless they accept the re*sponsor*bilities which recruiting brings, so let's develop this theme. The question of proper concern for your downlines comes under **A**ccountability, part of being a Leaders' **A**CTTER, which we will cover later (this is a variation of being an ACTTER that we covered in *Breakthrough Recruiting & Retailing*).

As a teacher and leader, you wield immense power. The minute you recruit someone, you get the power anyway; it is up to you whether you exercise it well, or badly, or not at all

---

That is the power to make below-par people average, average people good and good people fantastic. You have the power to turn failures into successes. That's a reason to love this business! But, if you do not practise your craft well, you may, instead, turn potential dream-creators into dream-dumpers. *People will fail because of you.*

No one actually wants their downlines to fail, so someone who misuses their power as a teacher and leader is not going to do it deliberately unless he or she is a total fool. So why do they do it?:

- They lack understanding ("No one explained to me how vital my role as a teacher and leader is to my people")
- They lack skill (they have not properly learnt what to do)
- They suffer from inertia ("I can't be bothered to do it right")
- They are unteachable.

Every distributor lost by a downliner is also one lost to you, costing you sales and new recruits which, because of the Geometric Progression, has an exponential effect on your business. For example, if your distributors average two new people each, and just one recruit fails due to of lack of support, that has actually lost you a total of *30 distributors* in just 4 levels! Count for yourself:

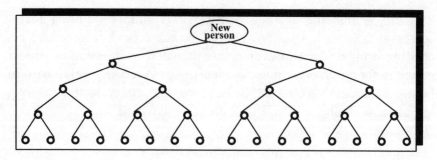

So it is well worth explaining to people why they should accept the responsibilities of teaching and leadership. And don't be afraid to make your views clear to a distributor who is letting down their group because they can't be bothered to accept re*sponsor*bility for their people's success, because you pay a big price for letting them.

5. Human nature is *A Pig*

The biggest problem I hear from leaders is that their people will not do what needs to be done. Leaders often blame themselves for this, so it is with a sigh of relief when they discover that they are not alone—*every* leader suffers in this way. That is why it is a *Pig*.

The fact is that, although *everyone* has dreams they would like to fulfil, few will ever do anything about it—that's human nature. As the story-teller in The City of Dreams story said, 'Had I offered them a magic carpet to take them there, *every single person in that audience would have climbed aboard.* But, left to themselves, few people will actually do anything about it.' (Chapter 6, *Get Off To A Winning Start*)

> *Hamish had fallen on hard times. His creditors were closing in on him. He realised that there was only one thing for it and that was to ask God to help him win the lottery. So he got down on his hands and knees and pleaded: 'Please God, help me. I'm in terrible financial trouble. I need to win the lottery. That's the only way out.' Nothing happened.*
>
> *Each day Hamish prayed, but still nothing happened. Each day he got more desperate until, one day, he cried out in despair: 'Please God! Do something! I'm desperate!'*

Back came an exasperated voice from on high:
'Hamish! At least meet Me half way! At least buy a
ticket!'

Many of your people will be desperate. Many will come to you for help but, like Hamish, they are not prepared to pay the price. God concentrates all the lottery winners on those who buy tickets and ignores the rest. You must do the same, but leave the door open because they may come back later. Unlike conventional business, your ticket office is never closed.

Every top group leader will tell you that in any meeting and training we only get through to a handful of people. The trouble is, we do not know which ones because only time will tell. Even by learning all the techniques in *The Secrets Series* and The STARS Leadership Programme, you and I will only reach only a few more people than the bad leaders and teachers, but that few could double, treble or quadruple your income.

6. The need to attract leaders is *A Pig*

This is also a distributor's *Pig*, as we covered in *Get Off To A Winning Start*. The size of your business and the speed of its growth will in the final analysis be limited by the number of winning leaders you have.

We have seen already that the industry relies too heavily on that very rare breed of person, the natural, charismatic leader. Top up-line leaders tell me that fewer than one in two thousand distributors have the natural leadership qualities to take them on a fast-track to the top without training.

So, unless you are willing to rely on finding that one person in two thousand, you need a way of turning ordinary people into leaders. The STARS Leadership Programme gives you the tools to do this.

7. Giving your leaders the wrong type of support

There are two sorts of leader—those with natural leadership abilities and those without—and you need to train and support them in very different ways.

The natural leaders

People with charisma pull everyone along behind them. They build big businesses quickly, usually breaking all the rules as they go. Though great at recruiting and public speaking, they are often useless at anything else. Although some combine their great motivational powers with the ability to teach, most are far too impatient to bother. But don't worry because, as I said earlier:

Never make the technique more important than the results

You are unlikely to be able to curb their natural, ebullient natures, and nor should you try: the cure could be worse than the disease. So, unless they have an appetite for it (and some do), it is unwise to subject them to the straitjacket of formal training.

A far better tactic is to recognise that such people are a big asset to your business. They could earn you a lot of royalty fast and will put a lot of *zing* into your motivational meetings. So why don't *you* take the responsibility of creating a team of teachers to give proper tuition to the people joining their fast growing businesses?

By no means all charismatic people succeed. They still need Focus and a Bulldozer Mentality, two of the Six Winning Attitudes—that is an inflexible rule which *no one* can break. So watch out for this. If you have a downline who is wasting their rare gift of charisma through lack of Focus and a Bulldozer Mentality, you will lose them unless you get them to use the techniques that are designed to help people into determined and purposeful Rocket Action.

Leaders without obvious leadership talents

Although structured training and leadership might stifle the tiny percentage of people with charisma, the complete opposite is the case with the rest of us: it is a disaster for us to try to get to the top without training.

Yet that, I am afraid, is what most of us try to do. Even with training we may find that, to compensate for lack of natural talent, as well as a Bulldozer Mentality we need more powerful Focus. Then you will be able to build a group as big as the next person.

~ ~ ~

Part II

Be A Winning Teacher!

*In this Part, we concentrate on the **teaching** aspects of your job as a distributor, as opposed to the leadership aspects. We will leave those to Part III.*

*Let me remind you that, although we are talking about teachers, distributors **are** teachers and teachers **are** distributors.*

*You only have to see the difference between a good distributor-teacher and a bad one to realise what a dramatic difference a few simple teaching skills **will** make to your business.*

There are teachers to whom all this comes naturally but not for most of us. It needs to be understood that a bad teacher does more harm than good and can actually cause failure. But a good teacher can often turn failure into success, and will make those distributors who are willing to learn even more successful even more quickly.

The teaching techniques I show you here can be used by you and anyone in your business. But first, let's answer the question: what is effective training?

≈CHAPTER 6≈

What Is Effective Training?

What follows is an actual interview. It is so representative of the way the great majority of experienced distributors have been taught that I think you will find it of great value.

Trainer Timothy is a great believer in training. I asked him how he trains his group.

'Well,' he said. 'I have training sessions after each BOM. I train my distributors in how to run their sizzle sessions. I spend a great deal of time on the phone telling people how to deal with situations that crop up. Everyone knows,' he added with great pride, 'that I have an open door any time for anyone who wants help. And I send regular newsletters to all my group—do you want to see one?'

I nodded, and was impressed by what I saw. Timothy knew how to do a good newsletter; it was packed with good tips. I made a mental note to ask him if I could borrow some of his ideas for myself.

I asked, 'How do you train your new people?'

'Although I say it myself, we are pretty strong there. Apart from the Strategy Meeting which every new distributor has, where we go through all the basics involved in getting their business going, we have Fast-Start Trainings every Saturday showing them exactly how to do their job. We cover things like suggested phone scripts—and, of course, a very simple One-to-One: Show the Product, Show the video, Invite the prospect to a BOM—you know the sort of thing.

'Then, once a month, we do an Advanced Training. And we run lots of seminars on the basic topics: recruiting, retailing and—most important of all—personal development. That's the real key! On top of that, we promote books, tapes, CDs and videos very hard. So you can see, our new distributors get a really good flying start. We tell them everything they need to know. If they can't make it after all that...... well...... they just haven't got what it takes!'

Timothy, like all good network marketeers, is very keen on training. I cannot fault him on his enthusiasm, his commitment and his determination to succeed.

Throughout the Programme, we stress that *Making sure people are accompanied in everything they do* is by far the most important form of training. Look again at what Timothy has said and you will notice that nowhere does he mention actually going out and *working with* his people. But it's not Timothy's fault because, following the Theory of Duplication, he is only following the example of his up-lines. And they, too, are merely doing what they were taught.

If the overwhelming majority of distributors think, as Timothy does, that it is enough to stop at telling people what to do, there must be a general misunderstanding about what is really needed. So let's spend some time looking at exactly what you should be doing.

There are two sorts of training:
- On-the-job training, accompanying people in everything they do
- Off-the-job training, or Arm's Length training.

Accompanying people in everything they do

This means rolling up your sleeves and actually doing the job on site with your people when they are:
- Making phone calls to prospects
- Retailing
- 2-2-2s
- Carrying out Registration and Strategy Meetings with their new people
- Running or sitting-in on sizzle sessions for their group (as opposed to your group)
- Completing administration
- Planning and targeting their time and work
- Showing them how to developing the right attitudes in response to practical situations and problems.

Arm's Length training means just what it says: covering the same activities as above but away from the job—i.e., in group sessions or trainings, in newsletters, over the phone, and in what are confusingly called "one-to-one" teaching sessions where you talk about the job without actually doing it together.

Sometimes, it can be difficult to tell whether a training session is on the job or Arm's Length. If a downline attends your sizzle session, you are giving them Arm's Length training; if you attend theirs to help them run it better, then you are giving them on-the-job training.

If everyone did what they were taught at Arm's Length trainings, *how much more successful would your group be?*

The trouble is, they don't, do they!

This is the point that little understood: *unless you make sure your people are accompanied in everything they do, there is little chance that what you teach will get done.* In other words, the effectiveness of intensive Arm's Length training without making sure that people are accompanied in everything they do is marginal at best.

In fact, if make sure that your people are accompanied in everything they do, you could entirely dispense with all *group* Arm's Length trainings (many excellent salesforces in conventional business do) and still end up with a far more highly trained group.

This may make you question the need for Arm's Length trainings. Well, *individual* Arm's Length trainings are important because you cannot be with everyone all the time, so you can "fill in" with phone calls, newsletters and those confusingly called "one-to-one" training meetings. *Group* Arm's Length trainings are important because:

1. They get your people together on a regular basis. This is an important part of the business and a very important tool for motivating in your group
2. They are very useful in supporting on-the-job training, provided that they are never done *instead of* people being accompanied in everything they do
3. They are an important part of Constant Repetition
4. The group discussions and the sharing of experiences possible in Arm's Length trainings are extremely valuable
5. They are indispensable to building teamwork, and network marketing is a teamwork exercise.

If you make two assumptions, you will not go far wrong:

- That, unless people are accompanied in everything they do, your people are not going to do the job in the way they are taught at Arm's Length trainings
- That the purpose of Arm's Length training is only to support people being accompanied in everything they do, not to be used instead of it.

Now let's look at what your aims should be as a teacher, because some of these may be different to what you might expect.

~ ~ ~

CHAPTER 7

What Does A Winning Teacher Want To Achieve?

The aim of teaching in traditional salesforces is to increase sales, but in network marketing, in which distributors do what they want to do, not what you would like them to do, this doesn't work.

In general, in network marketing, the only way to get more sales is to recruit more people.

Nor is the aim of teaching in network marketing to make people as good as they *can* be; not everyone wants to stretch themselves in this way. Many of your distributors will only want to be as good as they *need* to be to achieve their heart's desires, and they are just as much dream-creators as people who want to reach the top, because they are creating their own dream.

In network marketing, there are six objectives as a winning teacher:

1. To build up distributor numbers more quickly by reducing drop-outs
2. To help people get through their first six months
3. To help them develop Patience
4. To help those who drop out to recruit more people before they do
5. To help them turn dreams into reality
6. To help them turn lessons into habits.

1. To build the group more quickly by reducing drop-outs

Without proper tuition, most groups will contracting **Sponsoring Sieve Disease** (Chapter 9, *The Secrets Of Successful Recruiters*). Your group catches this when the "stream" of new distributors being poured into the "sieve" of your business is being matched by those flooding out of the bottom, and your group effectively stops growing.

This can occur with any size of group from two people to several thousand. If your group contracts this disease, at best your income will just stop growing. At worst, the disease will be terminal: your group will shrivel and die, sometimes frighteningly fast.

Actually, I prefer to think in terms of pouring fine wine into a sieve because distributors definitely are the fine wine of the business—difficult and time consuming to find with, just occasionally, a really good vintage turning up. Who would pour fine wine down the drain? Yet network marketeers do it regularly by recruiting people and then not giving them the best track to success.

The second consequence of recruiting without teaching is that, because it is so wasteful, you will soon run out of warm market contacts. You are then forced into advertising, leaflet distribution, cold mailing, buying lists of names, visiting trade shows, going out of your way to "pick up" strangers with a view to showing them the business, and any other ways you can think of to find new prospects.

Yet a Sponsoring Sieve is so easy to stop! As we saw, all you have to do is double-line your sieve to reduce the out-flow, first with Arm's Length training, and second by making sure that people are accompanied in everything they do.

Leaders are often excellent at Arm's Length training but it is usually the second liner, the really important one, that is missing.

2. To help people get through their first six months

The highest drop-out rate is during the first six months. Therefore, during this period you are not looking at how to help them to succeed, *you are looking at how to help them avoid failure* because it is not the things they are doing right that will get them through this period, it is:

- Avoiding doing the wrong things
- Learning to cope with problems……

…… that will get them through. Problems left unsolved are the ones that can grow to the point where they cause a person to drop out.

So be alert for any sign of someone going off track, and get them back onto the On-Track Path before it gets out of hand.

3. To help them develop Patience

Patience, as you know, is one of the Six Winning Attitudes. Network marketing, as we saw earlier in The STARS Leadership Programme, is not a sprint, it is a marathon. But it is a peculiar marathon in three ways:

1. The winner is not the first person to cross the line, it is everyone who does so, no matter how long it takes them
2. No one knows how long the race is. We all run the race blind, so that you only know it is over when you cross the winning line
3. This marathon has obstacles, but no one knows how many until they have finished the race. At each one, some distributors will fail. If the drop out rate is between 70% and 90%[1] overall, then between 10% and 30% will cross the winning line. If we take the 10% figure, the race might look something like this:

When distributors drop out of the race

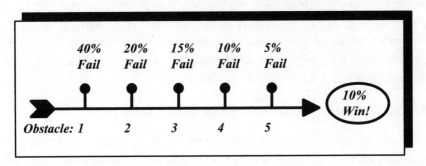

(Please note, these figures are for illustration only—and, of course, there are many more obstacles than five!)

What is so sad is that distributors drop out at what might have been their last serious obstacle. The moral must surely be:

Never give up, because your next serious obstacle could be the last!

---

[1]The drop out rate in some networks may be as low as 50%, but not in many

You will see that the drop-out rate is not even: it starts high and reduces dramatically with time. If you cascade the culture of making sure that people are accompanied in everything they do throughout your group and, particularly, use the All-Out Rocket Action Programme I will show you later in this book, you will smooth out this rate to your benefit because the longer people stay in the business, the less chance there is of them dropping out.

4. To help those who drop out to recruit more people before they do

Bearing in mind that 70% to 90% will fail, this is a huge resource lost unless you work as much of everyone's Contact List as you can as quickly as you can before they drop out.

This may sound cynical but in fact it is not: the *Urgency in Action* this makes you generate into every new distributor's business greatly reduces their chances of dropping out, and will result in you turning more people from dream-dumpers into dream-creators, which is the true measure of a great teacher.

But it has another important advantage. If a downline group has not established a working rapport with you then if a distributor drops out most of their group will go too. However, if you can work closely with a distributor's downline, you lessen the less chance of them following if he or she drops out.

5. To help them turn dreams into reality

The aim of teaching is not just to reduce drop-outs, to help people get through their first six months and to avoid a "knock-on" effect if a distributor drops out. Important though those are, the positive side of teaching is to help those distributors who stay to be as successful as they want to be. This is how you best apply the Keystone Law.

The success of every person, in whatever field of the professions, business, sport or art, has involved building, by accident or design, the same five stages. All five are necessary to the structure, and the strength of each is based directly on strength of the ones below, which is why we show them in the form of a pyramid. Adapted to our business, they make up **The STARS Pyramid to Success:**

SUCCESS!

Patience
To put no time
Limits on success.
To learn properly.
To teach and
lead properly

Commitment & Action
To do what is necessary.
No action = no commitment
because commitment *means*
determined, consistent *ACTION*

Enthusiasm
For your ATAC Lifeplan and heart's desires.
For the path you have chosen
(your business opportunity)

Conviction
That you can do it.
That what you are aiming for is right for you.
About network marketing, your company and your product

Knowledge & Understanding
Of yourself, network marketing,
your company, your product and its market.

What is the point of having the fastest racing car in the world if a tiny fault stops it from finishing the race? One loose connection is all that is needed to bring a mighty piece of machinery to a halt, and it is the same with a distributor's Pyramid to Success. In the same way as an athlete's body is only as strong as their weakest point, the strength of a distributor will be only as strong as their weakest stage, no matter how strong the other stages are.

To see how this works, take examples of success from your own life and notice how, by accident or design, you went through these five stages to get there. Then look at your failures and see which stage let you down. You will also see how that stage weakened all the ones above.

Therefore, you need to help a distributor you are working with build each stage as solidly as possible. That is the only way to ensure that the Pyramid to Success does not collapse into the rubble of failure.

The Pyramid to Success gives you an easy-to-follow trouble-shooting chart; if a distributor is not succeeding, you will be able to trace the problem to one or other of the stages. Once you know the cause, you can seek a cure.

6. To help them turn lessons into habits

As we saw earlier, the *only* purpose of knowledge is to help people to *do* better. But as a teacher you are not just imparting knowledge, you are creating habits of not just action but Rocket Action. Because only then will the person you are training continue to do the job in the way you have taught when you are not with them.

Now you know what your aims are as a winning teacher, how do you carry them out? This is the question we turn to next.

~ ~ ~

≈CHAPTER 8≈

The Steps To Being A Winning Teacher

The lazy way to being a winning teacher also happens to be the best! And that is to use *The Secrets Series* and The STARS Leadership Programme as your course material. If you keep referring a distributor you are with to the relevant sections, not only will you make your own job much easier but they'll soon pick up the habit and use it when they are in teaching mode.

However, you'll still need some skills to be a winning teacher.

First, be a Leaders' ACTTER!

ACTTER was covered in Chapter 4 of *Breakthrough Recruiting & Retailing*. However, to be a winning leader and teacher you need to become a slightly different ACTTER, and we call this **the Leaders' ACTTER:**

Be *A*CCOUNTABLE for helping them to succeed

We have a simple Code of Practice as network marketing teachers:

It is *your* responsibility to show a distributor what to do, but it is *their* responsibility what they do with it

---

Although you must do everything in your power to help someone who is on the On-Track Path, if they go off track because they are not following your advice, your responsibility is discharged.

*C*ONVICTION

Unless the person you are teaching is one of those very rare individuals who has the confidence and self-belief to get to the top with or without you, they need you to show Conviction not only in your own ability to teach them, but also in their ability to succeed— provided, of course, they follow the On-Track Path. This confidence is integral to their own belief.

Be *TEAM-MINDED*

This is the only major difference between being a standard ACTTER and being a Leaders' ACTTER, because Tell, not Sell does not apply to teaching and leadership.

Remember one of the rules:

Network marketing is a *teamwork* exercise. No one ever succeeded by not going to meetings

---

Make the person you are training feel welcomed as part of the team, especially at the start. Everyone likes to "belong", to feel wanted, to feel special. It is important to their success.

TRUTH = TRUST

The relationship between teacher and distributor has to be based on mutual Trust. Trust itself is of course based on truth.

ENJOY teaching! ENJOY meetings! ENJOY working!

Enjoyment is infectious. If you clearly enjoy the job, your distributor will learn far more because they enjoy learning from you!

RESPECT their views

If you respect the views of a distributor you are teaching, you will listen to them. Only by listening to what they have to say can you be sure that you are "pitching" your tuition in the best way for them.

But also respect their efforts. They may be doing a terrible job, but just remember that they doing the best they can, and anyone doing the best they can demands your respect.

So being a Leaders' ACTTER is:
- **A**ccountability
- **C**onviction
- **T**eam-minded
- **T**ruth = Trust
- **E**njoyment
- **R**espect.

Being a Leaders' ACTTER makes it easy for a distributor you are teaching to trust you, believe in you and want to follow your advice.

Second, KISS and Play CUPID!

We saw in Chapter 13 of *The Secrets of Successful Teachers & Leaders* that everything you teach must be capable of being put into practice by *The least experienced, least confident, least talented slowest learners* in your group, otherwise this is not a business for everyone. This means keeping everything as simple as possible and, as a teacher, you do this by KISSing and playing CUPID (Chapter 5, *Breakthrough Recruiting & Retailing*).

One reason why this is such a simple business is because it is very black and white: the distributor you are teaching is either committed enough to their success or they are not, they either have the right attitudes or they do not, they are either teachable or they are not, they are either on the On-Track Path or they are not. As soon as you introduce grey areas, you are already no longer KISSing.

Being a black and white business makes it easier to teach— provided you keep it black and white! Making sure that the distributor you are teaching understands that this is a black and white business requires a very straight-talking approach from you. Therefore, honesty and urgency are what they need: honesty so that they know exactly how they stand in relation to their own success or failure (black and white); and *Urgency In Action* to get the simple actions carried out.

To KISS in teaching, in other words to make it as easy as possible to understand, follow **The Steps of Training** in teaching situations:

The Steps of Training

Explain:
1. What to do
2. Why do it and
3. Why do it that way.

Show:
4. How to do it.

Check:
5. That they understand (i.e. check absorption)
6. That it is working (i.e. check effectiveness).

You do not necessarily need to go through the first four Steps of Training in the above order—that will depend on the circumstances. But you do need to develop the habit of going through *all* the Steps every time if you want your tuition to be as effective as possible.

You will notice from the Steps of Training that it is part of your job to make sure that the distributor you are with understands what they are being taught, and then check how it is working in the field. Believe it or not, these are steps often neglected by even the best professional trainers. I am the first to admit that I frequently go wrong on these points myself! It is very easy to assume that, because you know what you are talking about, the person you are teaching must have taken it in or that, because they seem to be doing it, it must be working. Neither is necessarily so.

Time spent in tuition is completely wasted if, at the end of it, a distributor has not understood what they are being taught or cannot make it work. So we should including these steps in our definition of teaching:

**Winning Teaching = Explaining + Showing
+ Testing Absorption
+ Checking Effectiveness**

...... and the best way to check absorption and check effectiveness is to observe someone as you work with them in the field.

Coach Charles is an athletics coach. I asked him if he used the Steps of Training.

'Exactly so,' he said. 'There is only one purpose in training—nothing else—and that is to help athletes to compete (in other words to apply the *How*) as well as they possibly can. To do this, we see the Steps of Training as a circle with all the other Steps contributing *directly* to doing *How* better.

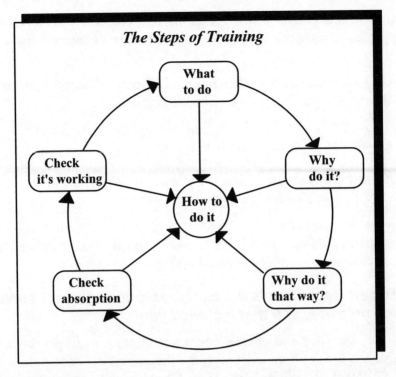

The Steps of Training

What to do

Why do it?

How to do it

Why do it that way?

Check it's working

Check absorption

'Seeing the Steps in this way keeps *you* as a coach, on track. It helps you check that anything you do will make your athlete perform better. If it does not, scrap it! But, of everything involved in training:

Without question the most important thing is to work with the athlete doing the job. All the valuable work is not in the classroom. it is *out in the field'*

The same applies to teaching your distributors. See *yourself* as a coach, and you will not go far wrong.

Third, use Constant Repetition......

We said that one of the aims of teaching is to create good habits of working:

Only when a lesson has become a habit in a distributor can you truly say, as a teacher, that it has been learnt

---

Constant Repetition, although it can be boring, is the only way to make sure that a lesson becomes a habit. Once it becomes a habit with them, the person you are teaching will constantly keep repeating the same message to their people—which is exactly what you want.

If you look again at our interview with Trainer Timothy, you will see that he is very strong on Constant Repetition.

Also, the only way to break a bad habit is by Constant Repetition of the good habit you want to replace it with.

Constant Repetition is the only way in which a slow learner or untalented person can learn

As a teacher, you can only make this is a business for all if you use Constant Repetition. If you don't, you'll turn it into a business for quick learners or naturally talented people.

Constant Repetition is the best insurance against people going off track, and that includes you!

It is very easy for a teacher to complicate things, to forget them or to give too much prominence to some things and not enough to others. Constant Repetition—re-reading books, re-listening to tapes and CDs, re-watching videos and attending meetings—will help you to keep on the On-Track Path. This is why at least half of your Thirty-Minutes-A-Day habit (Chapter 7, *Get Off To A Winning Start*) should still be devoted to recapping.

This is a very important lesson for you to teach the distributor you are training.

The STARS Teacher's Profile of Success

What makes a winning teacher? Someone who:
1. Has sufficient knowledge and understanding of their subject
2. Understands a distributor's needs
3. Has the *Patience* (one of the Six Winning Attitudes) to match their knowledge to a distributor's needs
4. Knows how to match their knowledge to a distributor's needs.

1. Knowledge and understanding of your subject. This will come if you have acquired the Thirty-Minutes-A-Day Habit and if you accept the need for Constant Repetition.

2. & 3. *Understanding a distributor's needs and having the patience to match your knowledge to their needs.* This will happen if you are a Leaders' ACTTER, KISS and play CUPID.

4. *Knowing how to match your knowledge to their needs.* If you follow the Steps of Training and you KISS and play CUPID, you will automatically match your knowledge to a distributor's needs. Then you need Constant Repetition (a) to get the message home, and (b) to make sure they don't stray off track afterwards.

These make up **The STARS Teacher's Profile of Success:**

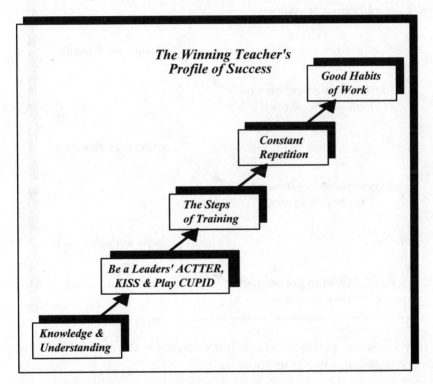

The Winning Teacher's Profile of Success

Good Habits of Work

Constant Repetition

The Steps of Training

Be a Leaders' ACTTER, KISS & Play CUPID

Knowledge & Understanding

How can you be Urgent *and* Patient?

I exhorted you to be *Urgent in Action* as part of having a Bulldozer Mentality—but I also counselled you to be Patient. This sounds contradictory, yet both are part of the Six Winning Attitudes. When should you be one, and when the other? In practice, it is easy.

When you are teaching someone, *Unfold at their speed* (part of KISSing and playing CUPID)—in other words, be Patient. But as soon as it is time for them to put learning into action, expect them to get on with it, which is *Urgency in Action*. Then, back to teaching and unfolding with Patience. Then, when it is time to put into practice what they have learnt, back to *Urgency in Action*. So, all the time you are working with someone, you are swinging from one to the other:

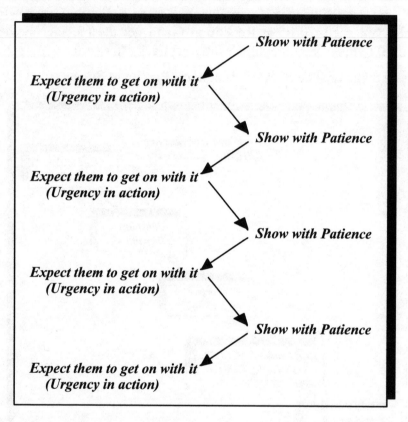

Now I'll show you how to teach a distributor the major techniques every distributor needs to know.

~ ~ ~

≈CHAPTER 9≈

How To Teach "People Buy People"

People Buy People is one of the Six Winning Attitudes because this is a people business, and how well the distributor you are working with will do will depend not on your product or plan, but almost entirely on how well they get on with people. You therefore need to teach them:

1. How to present *themselves* to prospects, customers and distributors already in their group
2. How to present the *product* (i.e., retailing) and the *opportunity*
3. How to be a leader of their group
4. How to teach their people the same.

The simpler you can make the path, the more the people who can follow you

---

1. How to present themselves

Keep It Simple! Show the distributor you are teaching how to become an ACTTER by using the text of Chapter 4 of *Breakthrough Recruiting & Retailing*.

2. How to present the product and the business

Teach them to KISS and play CUPID, which you can do straight from the text of Chapter 5 of *Breakthrough Recruiting & Retailing*.

3. How to be a leader of their group

Clearly, your new distributor does not know enough about the product and the opportunity to be able to teach it. They may also have no business or management experience and, indeed, little talent for it. Yet despite this, if they want to succeed, they must accept *immediate* responsibility for the success of the first people they recruit, in other words, to accept the responsibilities of leadership, otherwise their group may not get off the ground. But if someone does not know what they are doing, how can they possibly be expected to lead a group? The solution is simple; say to them, 'Will you make these four commitments?:

'1. *Support your uplines. They'll* do your leadership for you—if you let them! Encourage your people to learn the business properly by using all the trainings, meetings and other support your uplines and the company provide to make them, successful

'2. *Be a good example* to your people of how a good distributor should learn and do the job

'3. *Learn as a teacher.* But in your own time. Learning properly is what matters—so that you can teach your people right—not how long it takes [as we saw, this does not apply to people who need only a small group to earn the income they want]

'4. *Really, deeply care,* in your heart, about the success of your people. If you *really* care, then you'll do everything you can to help them.

'Is there anything here you find difficult? Yet that is all I need of you! If you just do this, you'll be discharging your responsibilities as a leader as well as it is possible to do!'

Finally, explain that, if they give you this commitment, *you* or one of their uplines will do the day-to-day leadership and teaching for them until such time as they wish to take on these responsibilities for themselves. Many never want to do this, and that is OK.

4. How to teach their people to do the same

All you want the distributor you are teaching to do is to pass your lessons onto their people, including the simple teaching techniques you show them. This involves showing them how to teach people to be an ACTTER, KISS and play CUPID, and in addition to be a Leaders' ACTTER and to follow the Steps of Training whenever they are teaching someone.

For by far the majority of your distributors (those who want to be led—Chapter 4: *What sort of distributors will make up your group?*), this is as far as they need or want to go. If the distributor you have been teaching wants to take the business more seriously, all you need do is show them how to use the relevant sections of The STARS Leadership Programme, but they will also need a more high flying upline to take them to the next level.

If you are that person, you can do it. But if their ambitions in the business are greater than yours and you don't wish to take them any further, introduce them to an active upline leader who will be more than happy to take them under their wing—as you know, finding active leaders is one of the *Pigs*, so upline group leaders are only too pleased to grab them!

Two areas of person-to-person communication require specific tuition: the Get-Active phone call and the 2-2-2.

1. The Get-Active phone call

Getting people to make Get-Active phone calls really is the big issue in network marketing.

We covered the basic Get-Active phone call in Chapter 11 of *Get Off To A Winning Start*. You can teach straight from that.

In your first session with a new distributor, explain the phone call, check for understanding and help them develop their scripts. Then make the first few calls for them, to show how it is done. It helps to fit a second phone to the socket using a double adaptor, so they can listen to both sides of the call (but they should not join in unless you ask them to).

As soon as they have the confidence, let them make a few calls and be very encouraging about their efforts; your new distributor is likely to be very sensitive at this stage. To avoid a situation of Dependency, let them make more and more of the calls as their confidence increases.

The fear of phoning is made much worse if a distributor you are working with is not *Focusing on their purposes* (Focus is one of the Six Winning Attitudes). Their aim is to make their ATAC Lifeplan and heart's desires a reality, but if they forget to focus on this the phone calls will become an end in themselves, and therefore much harder to make. You may find it helps them to read their Heart's Desires Card just before each phone call, or to prop a photograph of some important person or heart's desire by the phone.

Alternatively, you can use the Peter Bloomfield system (page 163) of making Get-Active calls.

It is easier for you if a distributor comes to your house to make the Get-Active phone calls, rather than you going to theirs. You can also work with more people because you are not wasting time travelling. Make sure they cover the cost of calls. However, if a distributor does not know you and your house does not reflect the image of a successful businessperson, go to theirs.

Don't forget the Chicken List!

We covered this in Chapter 3 of *The Secrets Of Successful Recruiters* and Appendix II of *Breakthrough Recruiting & Retailing*. You cannot afford to lose the hottest part of people's warm market. So, as soon as you feel confident enough to insist, only work with people who agree to include their Chicken List in their Contact List

2. The 2-2-2

We looked at the steps of the basic 2-2-2 in Chapter 12 of *Get Off To A Winning Start*, followed by the more sophisticated Reactive 2-2-2 in Chapter 13 of *Breakthrough Recruiting & Retailing*. These will allow you to gradually wean even the most inarticulate, inexperienced and slow learners into becoming competent at showing the business.

Again, don't introduce a new distributor to Reactive techniques until they are comfortable with the basic approach. The important thing is to play CUPID: let people learn at a pace at which they feel comfortable. To start with, you can conduct the whole 2-2-2 yourself. The system then allows you to give new distributors more to do in line with their increasing confidence. If you rush them, you risk losing them. But bring them in carefully and you may finish up with "Stars" who have the patience to become winning teachers themselves.

You will greatly accelerate the learning process if you show new distributors how to use a Presentation Folder in 2-2-2s (Chapter 5, *Breakthrough Recruiting & Retailing*).

~ ~ ~

≈CHAPTER 10≈

The Basis Of All Teaching: Accompanying People In Everything They Do

---

The single most important thing in network marketing is to make sure that people are accompanied in everything they do

---

That is why the concept is included in the On-Track Path.

Accompanying people in everything they do has already been extensively covered in the Programme, and you should re-familiarise yourself with all that has gone before. But it is so fundamental to your job that it deserves a closer look.

The biggest reason for failure

The biggest reason for failure is that distributors are either allowed to work on their own, or else they insist on doing so.

70% to 90% of your distributors will not succeed in network marketing on their own, but they may if they are accompanied in everything they do

---

The minute anyone works on their own, their talent, their Focus and their Bulldozer Mentality come an issue, and this no longer becomes a business in which anyone can succeed. So if you allow someone to work on their own, you are as a teacher predisposing them to failure. And if, despite your efforts, they insist on working on their own, they are predisposing themselves to failure. It's that important.

The way to get action

I expect you have already found how hard it is to get people to take action; yet nothing happens until they do! One way as we saw is to make them see an action as a "must". Another is to work with them on the job. If you can show them results from the actions you take together, this may motivate them to keep taking action after you have gone.

The way to develop faster

If you accompany someone in everything they do, they will develop many times faster than they will on their own. Even two *inexperienced* people accompanying each other in everything they do will develop at least five times faster than each trying on their own, quite apart from the obvious courage and mutual support they can give each other during those critical early days.

How to be the best they can be

If you want to make someone as good as they want to be as fast as possible (which surely is the point of the exercise), making sure that they are accompanied in everything they do is the *only* way in which this can be done.

Doing the job *is* teaching it, and teaching the job *is* doing it

The concept of accompanying people in everything they do applies the idea that doing the job and teaching it are inseparable. This is why I say in *Target Success!*: "Your Monthly Diary should *never* show you working on your own. *Every entry* should show you accompanying someone—upline, downline or crossline".

Produces a massive payoff for your business

Nothing would do more to reduce drop-out rates than making sure everyone is accompanied in everything they do, and just a tiny reduction in drop-out rate can have a truly massive payoff in terms of how your business builds. Let me give you an example, and to keep it simple I am going to make the following assumptions:

- That we start with a group of 100 people
- That the average drop-out rate of your group is 90% (drop-outs vary generally between 70% and 90%). So, out of every 100 distributors recruited into your group, 90 will drop out. This means that 10% (or ten out of every 100 recruited) are actively recruiting at any given time

- That your active distributors recruit an average of ten people during each sales period
- This chart does not represent any particular time-period. It could be one year or ten years—for the purposes of what we are talking about, it does not matter.

Given these parameters, the growth of the active distributors in your group will look like this (*each period starts with the same number of active distributors as there were at the end of the previous period*):

Group growth with 10% of distributors being active

Period	1	2	3	4	5	6
1. *Active distributors at start of period* ↓	10	20	40	80	160	320
2. *They recruit 10 new distributors each* ↓	100	200	400	800	1,600	3,200
3. *10% of these become active* ↓	10	20	40	80	160	320
4. *Active distributors at end of period*	20	40	80	160	320	640

Now let's explain this chart:

1. In Period 1, you start with 10 active distributors, being 10% of your group of 100 people
2. Those active distributors recruit 10 people each, making 100 new distributors in all
3. From those 100, 10% or 10 new active distributors will emerge
4. Add those to your original 10 active distributors, and you now have 20 active distributors in total your group
5. These start your Period 2
6. Now repeat this process to the end of Period 6.

Now, let's see what happens if, by making sure that people are accompanied in everything they do, you......

Reduce your group's inactive rate by just 1%: from 90% to 89%

Reducing your inactive rate by 1% seems hardly worth bothering with, does it? Yet, if you do that, your percentage of active distributors will go up not by 1%, but by *10%* (or from ten to eleven out of every 100 recruited).

You might think that this will give you a 10% increase in recruitment. But a network marketing business does not grow in a straight line, it grows on a Geometric Progression, and the results of that can be amazing (to make this conservative I have said that each active distributor still only recruits ten new people at each step):

Group growth with 11% of distributors being active

Period	*1*	*2*	*3*	*4*	*5*	*6*
1. *Active distributors at* start of period	*11*	*23*	*48*	*100*	*210*	*441*
2. *They recruit 10 new* distributors each	*110*	*230*	*480*	*1,000*	*2,100*	*4,411*
3. *11% of these become* active	*12*	*25*	*52*	*110*	*231*	*485*
4. *Active distributors at* end of period	*23*	*48*	*100*	*210*	*441*	*926*

Now compare this with the chart on the previous page and you'll see that, after six steps, you have finished up with 286 extra active distributors, an increase of 45%! Not bad for such an apparently insignificant decrease as 1% in the drop-out rate!

Some people may feel this comparison is unrealistic because they believe that active distributors are being required to recruit ten people off their own warm market lists in every sales period. Not so. If you follow The STARS Leadership Programme, each of your active distributors will be recruiting from the Contact Lists of some of the 89% or 90% who drop out (of course, before they drop out!), as part of accompanying them. If you feel that this figure is still too high, drop all the recruiting figures to five and you will see a similar pattern.

This chart is the best way I know to get the message across that making sure people are accompanied in everything they do is well worth doing even if the results seem insignificant at first. Just as with business-building, you need to fully understand the value of Patience in your teaching to give the Geometric Progression time to work.

How to introduce to your group the principle of making sure that people are accompanied in everything they do

If your group does not have the culture of making sure that people are accompanied in everything they do, you will find it very hard to get them to change their work habits. Remember the Theory of Duplication: *It is easier to change a good habit into a bad one than a bad habit into a good one*? Despite all the compelling arguments in favour of it and even though there is *not one* argument against, it will take Constant Repetition to get them to embrace a new way of working.

There is a slogan, *It is easier to give birth than to raise the dead,* meaning that it is very much easier to teach new people than to retrain your existing ones. You will have better results if you concentrate on introducing the concept to the new distributors coming into your group because, unless they have already been in another network, they will not yet have developed bad habits.

Having said that, don't neglect your existing people, because converting just one will make the exercise worthwhile, and if others see the results which that person can generate, they may follow suit. I suggest that you call your people to a meeting to discuss the subject.

Experienced distributors should also work with each other!

Making sure that people are accompanied in everything they do does not necessarily have to consist of a new distributor going out with an experienced upline or two inexperienced distributors going out with each other (the Buddy system). It could be two experienced distributors going out together to compare notes—this is an enormously valuable and much under-rated exercise! The distributors do not even have to be in the same paylines for both of them to receive great benefit.

What kind of teacher will you be?

If you wanted to be taught how to drive a car as well as possible in the shortest possible time, which instructor would you choose:

1. One who spent as much time as possible in the car with you
2. One who only came out with you for a couple of quick trips, then taught you at arm's length using the phone, books, classroom trainings and meetings
3. One who never gets into a car with you and did all their tuition using the phone, books, classroom trainings and meetings
4. One who did all their tuition by phone and the occasional meeting only?

I wonder if anyone would not agree that the best order is 1, 2, 3, 4? Yet the typical network marketing situation is 3 or 4 with, a long way back, 2 and, even further back, 1.

I hope you agree that 1 really is the teacher to be, and the only one who can genuinely call themselves a great teacher!

**Winning Teaching = Arm's Length training +
Accompanying people in everything they do**

Now you know the techniques you can use to make yourself a winning teacher, one thing is for sure: you do not want to waste your valuable talents trying to turn sows' ears into silk purses! So how do we avoid that?

~ ~ ~

≈CHAPTER 11≈

How Do You Choose Which Distributors To Work With?

As both a teacher and a leader, you are presumably hoping to run a business which you will want to make as profitable as possible. So to everything you do you should apply the normal business principle of assessing cost against benefit.

With who or what do you spend most time in your business? Your distributors. So isn't it even more important that you assess them, too, in terms of cost against benefit? Because, although you do not pay them to do a job, *they do cost you money*:

☹ They cost you money every time you see them

☹ They cost you money every time you speak to them on the phone

☹ They cost you money every time you think of them because, while you are thinking about them you are not thinking about your other distributors or other aspects of your business.

In fact, you may well be spending more time thinking about distributors who are not getting results than about those who are! And until you learn from your own experience, it is easy to waste a lot of valuable time and therefore money on people who will cost you rather than make profit for you.

Remember, too, that time given to undeserving people is time of which deserving people are deprived. That is not only unfair on them, it is unprofitable for you.

So how can we choose the right people to work with? The short answer is—to begin with, we can't. Remember the rule: *It is impossible to prejudge who will succeed and who will not,* so you give everyone the same and equal chance when they start, and then let them self-select into those who value your advice and act on it and those who do not.

The trouble with telling people not to prejudge is that it seems to fly in the face of logic. Logic suggests it should be possible to pre-judge, and further suggests that you should lean towards the ones with the "right" background or the "right" experience or the "right" Contact List or the "quick" learners. Or you might assume that the people who have obvious leadership qualities, who project themselves the best or who "talk the best act" are going to be your best bets. But:

"Talking a good act" is not the same as doing a good job.
So forget the good talkers and look for the good doers

Anyone can *talk* about what they are going to do. That's easy. It is much harder to actually go out and *do* it. The trouble is that, if you allow it to happen, the good talkers in your group will overshadow the good doers, so you need to be able to look past them to spot those often quieter people who are going to beaver away in your business.

If you cannot judge by the "obvious" qualities I mentioned above, what can you look for? All you need from a distributor you are choosing to work with are:

- **Do they want to succeed in network marketing?**
- **Have they a Hunger to Learn (one of the Six Winning Attitudes)?**
- **Will they apply what they have learnt?**

Why, as teachers, are we looking for these three particular attributes? Because *they are the **only** three things you cannot teach.*

Everything else a distributor needs, you can teach:
- *Anyone* can be taught to make Get-Active phone calls
- *Anyone* can be taught to show the business
- *Anyone* can be taught to retail
- *Anyone* can be taught the right attitudes
- *Anyone* can be taught to lead a group
- *Anyone* can be taught how to structure a group
- *Anyone* can be taught how to set targets and to plan

- *Anyone* can be taught to teach *anyone* else to do any of the above.

The only things you cannot teach are:
- The wish to choose network marketing as an occupation
- The willingness to learn
- The willingness to apply what they have learnt......

...... to people who do not want to do so—no matter how "right" their background, how "right" their experience, how "good" the people on their Contact List or how quick a learner they are.

This is another way of looking at the On-Track Path. Apart from anything else, you have a re*sponsor*bility to teach anyone who is On-Track, but these also happen to be the people where cost against benefit makes sense.

If anyone chooses to go off track, your responsibility to them is discharged and there is no benefit to the cost of supporting them, *so why keep letting them cost you money?* Leave them to their own devices—but of course leaving the door open for them to return.

Spend your time with your performers

The **80/20 Rule** applies to training just as it does to many other things. But in conventional business, it is the wrong way round: trainers spend 80% of their time with the worst 20% of their employees. So they spend the bulk of their time with their *non*-performers. That sounds crazy, but in fact it is the only way the traditional system will work.

In network marketing, the complete opposite rule should be applied. We should spend 80% our time with distributors who want to learn and only 20% with those who do not. And, as any trainer will tell you, the biggest kick comes from being with people who *want* to learn.

The other very big difference is that, whereas in traditional business the job of training is to make people achieve what the *company* wants out of them, in network marketing, your job as a winning teacher is to help people create their own dream: what *they want for themselves*. That, too, is much more satisfying.

What should you do about slow learners, untalented people or those who lack confidence in their ability?

Welcome them all! There may not appear to be much benefit against cost early on, but many of your best returns against investment will come from their ranks.

Give me one person who learns, no matter how slowly, rather 100 more talented people who do not. My experience in both sales and network marketing is that slow learners or less talented people are very often those who come out on top, *provided that they have Focus and a Bulldozer Mentality*. As we have said, there is nothing in network marketing that cannot be learned by anyone, so long as they give themselves the time.

Slow learners are less likely to forget

If a distributor has to struggle to learn, isn't it more likely to stick in their brain? *Easy come, easy go* applies just as much to gaining knowledge as it does to anything else.

Slow learners tend to have more patience

They say that good teachers make the best distributors and Patience (one of the Six Winning Attitudes) is essential to good teaching. Slow learners or less talented people, having had to struggle themselves, are more likely to sympathise with someone else who is struggling.

Slow learners are more likely to stay On-Track

People with quick minds or with talent are more likely to try to invent short-cuts or "better" ways of doing things, or to generally complicate the issue. Slow learners or less talented people are more likely to go unquestioningly down the success path you set out for them.

Where slow learners or less talented people are concerned, there is an extra responsibility to make sure that you set their minds at rest. You can do this very effectively with this six-point procedure:

1. Explain that there is *nothing* they cannot learn, *if they give themselves the time*
2. Point out the advantages we have just been discussing to show how they will eventually come into their own—perhaps after so-called "cleverer" people have dropped out
3. Get across the message that if, by perseverance, they create a good business with a high income when the "clever" people have dropped out, *who is the smarter person then?*
4. Make it clear that *This is not a sprint, it is a marathon*. Would they rather be in the lead at the end of the first lap, or win the race? Everyone who crosses the line by achieving what they want for themselves is a winner and, in marathons, people who set off too fast frequently fail to finish
5. Encourage them to *Put no time-limits on success* (Patience is one of the Six Winning Attitudes). At the end of the day, there are only those who make it and those who do not. Explain that every experienced network marketeer has seen the high-flyers

come charging in, quickly building huge balloon businesses and filling other, slower moving distributors with self-doubt. But a few months down the road, where are they then? Gone, while the more tenacious distributors are still there building cannonball businesses, slowly but solidly

6. Finally, guarantee your full support! Explain that you are so sure they are going to succeed that you are prepared to give them a lot of your very valuable time. You will help, advise and, most important of all, accompany them in everything they do—while, of course, they are on the On-Track Path.

To summarise: work hard for those who work hard for themselves

Irrespective of their experience and talent, the people who work hardest for themselves are the ones who will give you the greatest benefit against cost.

Having chosen the right people to work with, how much time should you give to each? We'll discuss that in the next chapter.

~ ~ ~

≈CHAPTER 12≈

How Much Tuition Does A New Distributor Need?

The amount of tuition needed varies enormously from person to person. In this respect, you will find your distributors come in with three different attitudes to sales:
- Those who want to *Sell the deal*
- Those who are ACTTERs—they want to help people
- Those with no idea what to do.

Those who want to *Sell the deal*

These are generally traditionally trained salespeople, entrepreneurs and people with positive, outgoing, perhaps competitive personalities.

It is common for new distributors to prejudge such people as the ones to "home in" on as their first recruits. You will need to warn them not to do this because people who set out to *Sell the deal* are, if anything, less likely to succeed (Chapter 8, *Breakthrough Recruiting & Retailing*). So you will need to teach them to back off. Instead of "selling", they will need to learn to "show", "invite", or "share" (whichever word you like to use).

It is particularly difficult to teach traditionally trained salespeople to do this because you are trying to change a totally different philosophy of selling that may have become a deeply ingrained habit, and which departs from being an ACTTER in just about every way you can think of. The trouble is that if they don't learn they will in turn treat their distributors as traditional salespeople—thus mistraining one complete leg of your business—usually with disastrous results. So I would not spend too much time on them unless they are prepared to learn to *show* rather than *sell*.

However, if you can convert an experienced salesperson to being an ACTTER, you are likely to have a real "Star" in your business, partly because they will find that showing is much easier than the selling they are used to, and partly because they can then use their previous experience and skill to advantage.

The ACTTERs. They want to help people

Among others, you will find that creatively (as opposed to traditionally) trained salespeople are normally already ACTTERs. They need very little tuition because they are already very close to the network marketing way of doing things:

Creatively trained salespeople are taught to make friends of their customers, whereas distributors in network marketing are taught to make customers of their friends

---

...... As you can see, not much difference. Both techniques mean learning to *Show not Sell*; so creative salespeople have already, without knowing it, learnt to become ACTTERs. This does not mean that they are any more likely to succeed, but they will need less tuition.

Other people who are already likely to be ACTTERs are helping professionals such as nurses, teachers and social workers, and people who have been properly trained to deal with the general public: receptionists and telephonists, retailers and retail assistants, and so on. They will quickly learn how to present themselves, the product and the business.

Those with no idea what to do

These will be the majority of your distributors. They are not used to dealing with the general public and they may find showing the product and the opportunity very difficult to start with. Less obvious examples of people who may have no idea what to do are educated, intelligent people like professionals, some company directors, managers and technicians, who have not learnt how to deal with people in the right way.

Experience shows that people who come in with no idea of what to do stand every bit as much a chance of success as those in the two earlier categories, because they are often the most teachable ("If people *know* they don't know, they can be taught; if people *think* they know, they can't"). People with business or sales experience can have so many preconceptions about how things should be done that they have become unteachable.

How many 2-2-2s should you do with a new person?

Let's deal with the theory first, and the theory is: *Do as many as are necessary!*

With people who want to *Sell the deal*, you will only need to do a few before they either grasp the "showing" rather than "selling" approach or prove to be unteachable. If they prove to be unteachable, don't waste any more of your time.

You will need to do even fewer 2-2-2s with *creatively* trained salespeople because they are already used to presenting both themselves and their product in a network marketing way. They have already become ACTTERs without realising it.

The normal practice with uplines, if they do 2-2-2s at all, is to do just enough with a new distributor to allow them to go out on their own. Then, in their haste to cram as many new distributors into their business as they can, they go charging off to rush someone else through a couple of 2-2-2s.

It may seem that judging them ready to go out on their own is the right yardstick. *But it isn't.* Remember that this is a *teaching* business. Although a new distributor may be good enough to go out on their own:

Do they know enough yet to teach their new distributors as well as *you* could teach them?

It is not your standards and techniques but the standards and techniques of your new distributor that will cascade down *their* leg of *your* business. Looked at in this way, are you still satisfied that your new distributor has learnt enough to teach your people properly?

So the main purpose of doing 2-2-2s is not to make sure your distributors know how to show the business.

The purpose of 2-2-2s is to make sure that they know enough to teach their people to show the business to at least the same standards as yourself

---

Only in this way can you ensure that your standards and techniques reach undiluted to the bottom of your business.

On this basis, it is hard to think that even the best new distributor would need fewer than five 2-2-2s. Someone who is not used to dealing with the public, is a slow learner and perhaps lacks confidence as well, will need...... how many? ...... As many as it takes!

That is the theory. The reality is that a good and conscientious teacher can almost never do as many 2-2-2s as they would like with a new distributor. The minute the new distributor has two people signed into their group, you are going to have to let them accompany one in everything they do while you do the same with the other. The option of *Three*-to-Ones is not acceptable: that really is a bit much for most prospects!

This makes it very important that you talk through, by phone or in person, *every* 2-2-2 an inexperienced distributor makes with their people, and every session of Get-Active phone calls they have with their downlines, as well as discussing in detail the advice they are giving to their people.

Of course, the people a new distributor brings in will be almost as inexperienced as they are. So you will also have to talk through the same three topics (2-2-2s, Get-Active phone call sessions and the advice they want to give to their people) with them, too, until the original distributor is experienced enough to take over.

Now we, as teachers, are getting moving. So let's see in the next chapter how you can Fast-Track a new distributor into action and early success.

~   ~   ~

≈CHAPTER 13≈

How To Lock In New Distributors

The way to lock a new distributor in is actually to find ways of stopping them from dropping out, as we saw earlier. So now we'll look at why someone you are working with might drop out, and how we can avoid that. Five significant causes of drop-out are:

1. Lack of early results
2. Going off track at the start
3. Failing to create momentum in their group
4. Having too much time to think
5. Lack of a Bulldozer Mentality.

1. Lack of early results

Urgency in Action applies as much to how you start a new distributor as to how you act in your own business. And there is nothing like *success in action* for making them want to do more and better.

A little personal success is better than one thousand words or one hundred examples of other people's success

---

The worst delay can occur at the beginning. No matter how long it took them to make up their minds, as soon as someone signs up they want to get going. Then you make them wait one or two weeks while their starter kits and samples arrive!

The quickest way to get your new distributor started is:

- Have spare starter kits and samples on hand to get them going straightaway
- Arrange the earliest date you can for their Strategy Meeting (*The Distributor's Action Plan* and Appendix II, *Breakthrough Recruiting & Retailing*)
- Get them booked into the first available training
- Get them to the next sizzle session, yours or an upline's
- Take them to the next BOM (if your company promotes them)

- Lend them a book, tape, CD or video—but don't overdo this! Remember C**U**PID: *Unfold in Bite-Sized Chunks*, so give them enough to keep them occupied but not enough to put them off. They can always come back for more

- Make the first Get-Active phone calls with them as soon as possible—the best time is immediately after the Strategy Meeting. The sooner the first 2-2-2s are booked and they sign up their first distributors, the less chance of dropping out.

2. Going off track at the start

If your new distributor starts on the On-Track Path, you have a chance of keeping them on it. If they start off track, it is very difficult to get them to change because bad habits and wrong conceptions are already becoming ingrained. As the theory of Duplication states, *It is easier to change good habits to bad ones than bad habits to good ones.* So first:

KISS and keep it achievable

The harder you make it for your new distributor to copy what you do, the more chance they will drop out. They also need to feel that they can achieve their heart's desires because, again, once they stop believing in that, they will drop out.

Get them into the learning habit straight away

As a syllabus, introduce your new distributor to the Learning LAWR as soon as you can (Chapter 7, *Get Off To A Winning Start*).

Explain that *They are on a six months' apprenticeship*, and during that six months they must not be too concerned about their results, only about building for the future. Ask them: *Is it worth this to achieve what they want from the business? Is it worth this to make their ATAC Lifeplan and heart's desires a reality? In what other business does it take only six months to learn how to earn enough to retire in a few short years?*

You may find a problem in getting a distributor to read. If so, when they ask for advice, point them to a relevant chapter or page in a book, ask them to read it and then get back to you if that doesn't solve the problem. With those who will do it (not all will, but they are not going to last anyway), it will very much streamline and accelerate their learning and take a lot of work off your hands, allowing you to get on with other things. It is also very duplicatable.

Even if they have a genuine literacy problem, your message must be clear: if they want to be as good as they can be, reading is essential. Tapes, CDs and videos are not substitutes for reading (Chapter 7, *Get Off To A Winning Start*). I have found, time and again, distributors with reading problems whose abilities have improved dramatically because they took my advice and trained themselves to develop a reading habit, starting with just a few pages a day. If even this is impossible, help them to find professional help. For distributors with a Bulldozer Mentality, the enormous benefits of learning to read network marketing and personal development books may be just the motivation they need to improve their literacy!

Reluctant readers soon become converts to reading when they find that much the quickest and easiest way to teach their people is to refer them to written texts. But you have to get them to that point.

There is a very important point here:

Don't base your decisions on what dream-dumpers won't do, base them on what dream-creators need to do, then encourage the dream-dumpers to follow suit

---

...... because your dream-creators will read anything they can get their hands on if you show them how it might accelerate them on their path to success and help their people to do better.

Stress the importance of A Hunger to Learn

A Hunger to Learn is one of the Six Winning Attitudes. But the little food of thirty minutes a day study will only satisfy their theoretical knowledge needs. It will not develop the practical knowledge they will require to succeed. And someone you are teaching will only acquire this is you can show them that:

Every **situation is a learning situation, if they let it be so**

---

3. Failing to create momentum in their group

Until a distributor you are working with gets group momentum going, they are always at risk of dropping out. Once they have momentum going, they are extremely unlikely to do so. By far the best course of action is to make sure that they are intensively worked with (provided they are on the On-Track Path) until they have got momentum going, even if this takes several months.

Don't assume that because a new distributor gets good early results, they have generated ongoing momentum, because sometimes an early surge fizzles out. They can only be said to have ongoing momentum when they have one or more anchored legs. What this means and how to anchor a leg are explained on page 154.

4. Having too much time to think

If you give a new distributor too much time to think, real or imaginary doubts can grow and fester at frightening speed. Work on the principle that, if they have things to do, they won't have time to worry.

Apart from getting them started quickly in the way we saw earlier, any action you take to fast-track them—including the fast recruiting techniques in *The Distributor's Action Plan*, Chapter 14 of *Breakthrough Recruiting & Retailing* and Chapter 22 of this book—will automatically help to overcome this problem.

5. Lack of a Bulldozer Mentality

You'll notice that the four reasons for drop-out we have looked at so far can all be put down to bad teaching, although in fairness that is often due to a new distributor rejecting upline support.

Lack of a Bulldozer Mentality, however, a very major cause of drop-out, is down to their attitude. There are things you can do about this, but it is such a big subject that I will devote the next chapter to it.

~ ~ ~

CHAPTER 14

Teaching A Bulldozer Mentality

A Bulldozer Mentality is a habitual way to react to difficult circumstances in a positive, determined, "unstoppable" way

---

Having a Bulldozer Mentality is one of the two most important of the Six Winning Attitudes. Desire and Focus on that desire are what create a Bulldozer Mentality, whereas *Urgency in Action* is how you express it from day-to-day.

The best antidote to dropping out is having a Bulldozer Mentality. You need to get the message across to a distributor that, if they keep going for long enough, they simply must succeed! You also need to get across just how important having a Bulldozer Mentality is: *That no amount of knowledge, talent or support will ever make up for not having a Bulldozer Mentality.*

If the distributor you are teaching is allowing you or someone to accompany them in everything they do, how strong a Bulldozer Mentality they have is not so much of an issue. But it becomes a serious issue if they insist on working on their own: one reason for an 80% failure rate is that they did not have a Bulldozer Mentality.

A Bulldozer Mentality is a compensation mechanism given to us by God or Nature to overcome obstacles. People who have one often acquired it early in life when they found that, with it, they could compete successfully against those with more natural ability.

Because it is normally developed as a response to problems, if you are teaching a talented distributor it is possible that they have not developed a Bulldozer Mentality because their advantages may have allowed them to coast through their early years with less effort. This is why people who have both a Bulldozer Mentality and a lot of talent are rare, fortunately for us lesser mortals! The rest, when they get out into the wide world only to find that talent by itself is not enough to get them to the top, often find themselves giving way to less talented people.

One reason why people do not develop a Bulldozer Mentality later in life is because they do not realise they can do so; the tendency is to see it as an attribute, not a habit which can be learnt, and I will show you ten proven ways to help a distributor develop it:

1. Enjoying the business
2. Having Pride and Conviction
3. Having crystal-clear heart's desires
4. Having clear satisfactions from work
5. Getting quick, early results
6. Treating this business with the seriousness it deserves
7. Learning the value of Patience
8. Treating the business as their last chance
9. Knowing about *The Pigs Around The Corner*
10. Taking the responsibilities of teaching and leading seriously.

1. Enjoying the business

Enjoyment is part of both being an ACTTER and a Leaders' ACTTER, and its role in creating a Bulldozer Mentality is another reason why it is so important (Chapter 4, *Breakthrough Recruiting & Retailing*).

If a person *enjoys* doing something enough, how important is having a Bulldozer Mentality?

So the more you can create an exciting, enjoyable atmosphere around a distributor you are teaching, the less they will need to rely on grim determination.

2. Having Pride and Conviction in the business

Pride is one of the Six Winning Attitudes, and Conviction is part of being an ACTTER. Both have been well covered in The STARS Leadership Programme.

If a distributor has pride and conviction in what they are doing, how much of a Bulldozer Mentality will they need?

Pride and conviction are also strong defences against doubts, set-backs, uninformed media coverage, or failed distributors who attack network marketing or try to shift the blame for their own failures onto their sponsors.

3. Having crystal-clear heart's desires

If a distributor wants something badly enough, won't that give them the Bulldozer Mentality to keep going?

If you can help them find heart's desires that *really* turn them on, would you need to work at motivating them, *or would you just point them in the right direction and watch them go?*

You will have much more success with a distributor if you believe that keeping them *Focused on their purposes* (Focus is one of the Six Winning Attitudes) is much more important than showing them how to succeed as a distributor. *Showing* people what to do is easy; *motivating* them to do it is the problem, and this is where the ATAC Lifeplan and Heart's Desires Card help. Even though this appears to be blindingly obvious, it can be difficult to persuade people how important crystal-clear heart's desires are to their success, so I'll show you how to deal with a couple of typical reactions:

"Goal-setting is American, a bit over the top or 'hypy'"

Even if someone doesn't accept the need for goal-setting, few would dispute that:

No matter how well someone has done up to now, they would have got further faster, and dealt with more obstacles more easily *and with more enthusiasm,* if they had set purposes to go for

---

Words do matter, so stop using the word goals and start using purposes or heart's desires.

"I am very self-motivated. Setting goals is not going to make me work any harder!"

This is the person you really want in your business, because they are so self-motivated and not afraid to work! But you may find they have not attracted the success their hard work deserves, and that is precisely because they have not set goals. The result is that instead of focusing on the outcome—what they want from life—they have focused on the satisfaction of work itself. So they dissipate their potential in Catherine wheel actions.

They misunderstand that, for someone like themselves, the reason for having purposes is not to *motivate*, it is to get them to change their *focus* away from work and onto the outcome they want from work, to change them from a Catherine wheel to a rocket. So you need to explain this to them. You may find that what we call **The Focus Equals Outcome Ladder** will help you to do this:

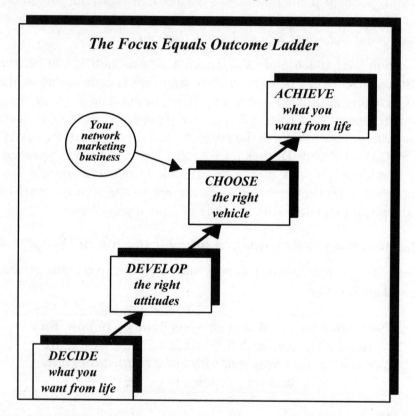

This is what the distributor you are working with probably doesn't understand:

Purposes both *start* and *finish* the process of achieving them

The steps they will go through whenever they do something are:

1. Decide what they want to achieve
2. Develop the attitude to achieve it
3. Choose the vehicle—in other words, how they are going to achieve it
4. Achieve what they set out to achieve.

This is how they carry out every task they do, even the simplest everyday one. To show how it works, suggest that they see how far they can get in making a cup of tea without following these steps! Yet when it comes to work, people hardly ever use that as a vehicle for getting what they *really* want from life, whatever that might be.

You can now see why some self-motivated people never seem to achieve what they should: they have got the two middle bits of the Focus Equals Outcome Ladder right, but it is the two ends that are missing. So they squander their hard work and time on tasks that lead nowhere.

Most jobs barely sustain people in a particular lifestyle which is why someone coined the phrase: **J-O-B = Just Over Broke**—or as we say, too much month at the end of the money. That is all that most people ever achieve. Now, in network marketing, they have the opportunity to do more—to get what they want from life. But they will only do so if you help them to decide what that is.

If you ask a distributor you are teaching what their aims and ambitions are, they will usually reply within the restrictions of what they believe they could *actually* afford or *realistically* achieve. This may not be what they would really, deep-down, like to accomplish. But what, they think, is the point of telling you some secret desire when they know they will never in a million years be able to achieve it? So what they give may be a compromise desire—in other words, something they think is within the limit of their attainment and, at the same time, something they think you will not find laughable or unrealistic. The trouble is:

A compromise desire is almost never hot enough to truly motivate a person to achieve it

---

So you may have to remove barriers that your distributor has created in their own mind against daring to admit, perhaps even to themselves, what their heart's desires really are. The way to do this is to:

1. Create trust between you. If you are a Leaders' ACTTER, you will already have done this

2. Make sure they understand the importance of having purposes to achieve, but that these must be truly heart's desires otherwise the system won't work

3. Create a framework within which they can really let their imaginations run riot. One way is to share with them your ATAC Lifeplan and Heart's Desires Card: 'This is why I am here. Why are you here?'

The techniques of goal-setting are covered in a variety of ways throughout *The Secrets Series* and The STARS Leadership Programme. In addition to that, they are an integral part of personal development and worth your while as a teacher to study in depth.

Some teachers ask distributors to practise goal-setting even though they do not do it themselves. This is a clear case of trying to sidestep the Theory of Duplication which states, *People tend to copy what you do, not do what you say.* As I said before, *Practise what you preach!* So, if you have not already written out your ATAC Lifeplan and Heart's Desires Card, start with yourself!

4. Having clear satisfactions from work

Many occupations can be carried out well enough even though the person hates what they are doing. This is not so with network marketing: no one can be even an adequate distributor unless they get some clear satisfactions from doing the job. It will reinforce your distributor's Bulldozer Mentality if you help them to isolate what satisfactions they get and ask them to contemplate them for only a few minutes a day. What does satisfaction at work mean to people? Everyone is different, but here are some ideas as to what it may mean:

- Getting enjoyment from their day-to-day activities
- Pride in themselves for a job well done
- The respect of family, friends, customers, people who work for them, bosses, competitors or the industry for being good at what they do

- Creating or maintaining the lifestyle they want for themselves or their family
- Helping people (customers, downlines) through what they do
- A sense of mission, a sense of destiny or a crusading zeal for what they can achieve through what they do.

As you can see, this is quite different from seeking purposes to achieve and, unlike heart's desires which you have to distil down to very few:

The more satisfactions a distributor can find for doing what they do, the more motivated they will be to do it.

---

5. Getting quick, early results

We have already covered this in Chapter 13.

6. Treating the business with the seriousness it deserves

Network marketing has perhaps the lowest entry requirement of any potentially high-level business or career. You need no qualifications or experience, little talent, only a minimal investment, no selection procedure or interview to pass, and you can start straightaway.

Many other businesses require a lot of time, red tape and effort just to get to the starting gate; going to all that trouble in itself creates the Bulldozer Mentality needed to make the business succeed. If you want a job, just getting through the selection procedure can be extremely tough. But, with network marketing, starting up is all too easy and this can generate a feeling of *Easy come, easy go.* So one of the penalties of the low entry requirement is that it actually helps people to fail because they do not take the business seriously enough.

To show you how the ease of entry can undermine your Bulldozer Mentality, let me ask you a question:

> *'If you had invested £100,000 in your network*
> *marketing business and put your house on the line,*
> *and had just spent six months' hard work wrestling*
> *with bank managers, lawyers, estate agents, local*
> *government "officiousals" and "uncivil" servants,*

recruiting and managing staff, briefing printers, negotiating with suppliers and dealing with utility companies just to get started, would you be working harder right now?'

The only people I have found to honestly answer 'No' to this question are those who eventually succeeded. *They succeeded because they **did** take the business as seriously as they could, right from the start.*

Now, if you are reading this, the chances are that you are a motivated person who has come into network marketing with every intention of doing whatever it takes to succeed and you probably believed, up to now, that you were putting in all the effort you could, even if you are part-time. If a determined person like yourself would actually have worked harder if *you* had invested all that money and effort, *what effect do you think the low cost and ease of entry are having on the levels of determination and commitment of a distributor you are teaching who is, perhaps less ambitious, than you are?*

But, before I show you how to tackle this problem, here is another side of the same coin......

7. Learning the value of Patience

Patience is one of the Six Winning Attitudes. People often drop out due to impatience. They want results yesterday and, when these do not come, they drop out. Yet many people look to network marketing as the answer to some serious problems in their lives, and for that it deserves great respect—respect which they are not giving, because it has been too easy to start the business.

A good question to ask at trainings is whether anyone there has started a new business that involved borrowing money and putting their houses on the line. There almost always is. Then ask how long they were prepared to wait before they broke even or got into profit. A typical answer is two or three years.

People who borrow money and put their houses at risk will wait for over two years to see results; yet network marketeers who borrow no money, do not have to put up their houses as security *and* have far bigger rewards to go for, give up after days, weeks or months! If such a big reward is on offer, isn't it worth exercising a bit of patience?

To deal with this problem and the previous one of not taking the business seriously enough, get a distributor you are working with to change their conception of the business. Instead of measuring the business by what it cost, get them to quantify it in terms of *what they can get out of it*. For instance:

Network marketing is perhaps the only way for them to make their ATAC Lifeplan a reality

Show them how to value their business, not by what it costs to join and run, but by the purposes they can achieve through it—in other words, making their ATAC Lifeplan and heart's desires a reality.

Money or status—two ways to value the business

We are all motivated by the wish to earn the money we need to lead the lifestyle we want. Ask the distributor you are teaching to place that value on their business. For instance, if they need to earn £30,000 a year to sustain their lifestyle, theirs is a £30,000 business.

Or the distributor you are teaching may be more interested in **status** than money. If so, this can mean two things to them: having a high position on the compensation plan or "employing" a large number of people (i.e., distributors) in their business.

If they see status in terms of their position in the compensation plan, keep reminding them that they can reach the top position in the network within one to five years from starting. But ask how long, if ever, it would take them to reach the status of a top position in any other career open to them.

If what motivates them is being able to say that they have, for example, 500 or 5,000 distributors in their group, focus them on the fact that this is the value they should place on their business.

Of course, someone you are teaching may be motivated by more than one of these attractions. The important thing is to find out what will excite them about the business or the purposes they can achieve through it, then educate them to value the business in these terms. They must get rid of, once and for all, the *Easy come, easy go* attitude that stops them from taking network marketing seriously.

8. Treating the business as their last chance

How much of a Bulldozer Mentality would a distributor have if they really believed that this was their last chance?

This is perhaps the classic example of how to turn the need for action into a "must", which, as we saw before, is the way to get the person you are teaching to take action.

In many cases, it may not be too far from the truth to say that this is the last *realistic* chance for a distributor: if they are a redundant executive whose only crime is that they are over 40, or bankrupt and unable to get credit or finance, or a woman returning to work after 20 years of parenting, or for someone who has no other realistic way of creating the income they need.

Even if the distributor you are working with is really committed, the comfort of knowing that they have other options will take at least some of the edge off their focus and performance. So you will do them a favour if you can get them to behave as if they really do have nowhere else to go if this business does not succeed for them.

Motivational cards really work, but British people in particular feel self-conscious about using them—in this instance a card in the bedroom, on the bathroom mirror, on the sun visor of the car and inside the lid of a brief-case, saying, **"THIS IS MY LAST CHANCE!!"**

However, if they see you are not self-conscious about using them, some of them might do the same.

9. Knowing about *The Pigs Around The Corner*

The Pigs Around The Corner were covered in detail in Chapter 5 of *Get Off To A Winning Start*. If people are warned about a problem and therefore prepared for it, they are far less likely to give into it.

10. Taking the responsibilities of teaching and leadership seriously

Many people find it difficult to motivate themselves. But put a *responsible* person into a training and leadership role and they will find reserves of determination and toughness they never knew they had. Point out to a distributor you are working with that they will make or break other people by their own example, and they might rise to the challenge. Don't be frightened to do this—people who do not rise to the occasion will not survive anyway.

There is only one reason for having a Bulldozer Mentality, and that is to help people overcome problems...... problems...... problems...... Let's look at ways to deal with these in the next chapter.

~ ~ ~

≈CHAPTER 15≈

Problems...... Problems......Problems— And Teaching How To Overcome Them

This chapter is extremely important to you as a teacher because the only reason a distributor of yours will drop out is because of problems—unless, of course, network marketing is simply the wrong occupation for them to be involved in. Some problems are self-inflicted—like the refusal to learn or to apply what they have learnt. Others are barriers imposed by circumstances which distributors come across as they build their business.

As with a Bulldozer Mentality, problems are much less of a factor if the distributor you are teaching allows you or someone to accompany them in everything they do. Problems become much more serious if they insist on working on their own.

In fact, there are only a tiny number of problems that cannot be overcome successfully by almost every distributor if they go about it in the right way, and you play a big part in helping them do this. Almost any problem encountered in network marketing will have already been dealt with successfully by literally hundreds of thousands, if not millions, of distributors the world over.

So, although most people see a problem as the cause of failure, it is not. Given that the great majority of distributors have the ability to overcome it, it follows that:

Failure is not caused by a problem. It is caused by your distributor having *insufficient personal motivation* to overcome the problem.

Why do we have problems?

Because they help us develop our capabilities! Unquestionably, adversity is the best teacher. The overwhelming reason why people improve is because they have to, to overcome a problem, or want to, to prepare themselves for the greater problems that will stand in the way of greater achievement. If people got what they wanted when they wanted, without the need to improve, most people would never develop themselves. Seen in this way:

Problems are lessons in disguise

Met in the right way, life's difficulties and troubles don't slow us up, they actually speed us to our purposes because they spur us to call into play new forces and powers to overcome them—forces and powers which we can then use to help us on the rest of our journey.

Therefore, the trick is to show the distributor you are working with to see problems as giving them opportunities to develop themselves. So whenever a problem occurs, teach your distributor to ask:

"What is this problem trying to teach me?"

Develop their Bulldozer Mentality

As I said earlier, the only purpose of having a Bulldozer Mentality is to help people overcome problems. The more you can help your distributors to develop that ability (as we discussed in the previous chapter), the less likely they will be to drop out.

Forewarned is forearmed

The impact of a problem is greatly magnified if it is unexpected. Indeed, the unexpectedness of a problem can be very much worse than the problem itself. Good sailors do not fear rough seas or high winds; it is the more modest wave or gust of wind catching them unawares that is the real danger.

This means that a distributor of yours needs a stronger Bulldozer Mentality to overcome an unexpected problem than to deal with an expected one. Therefore it is an important part of your job as a teacher to tell them what problems to expect and to give them strategies to deal with them when they occur. This is why we isolate the problems consistently faced by every distributor as *Pigs Around The Corner* (Chapter 5, *Get Off To A Winning Start*. The "Pigs" for leaders and teachers are covered in Chapter 5 of this book).

The "Nos": fear of rejection

Fear of rejection is one of the hardest problems a distributor has to deal with, which is why it is one of *The Pigs Around The Corner*. You'll find strategies for dealing with rejection all the way through *The Secrets Series* and The STARS Leadership Programme, and you should familiarise yourself with them. But I'll highlight one or two points for you.

Successful distributors are simply those who accept more "Nos" than unsuccessful ones

---

A rejection is related to not getting a "Yes". But in network marketing the distributor you are teaching is not after "Yes's":

All they want are decisions from their prospects and it does not matter whether those decisions are "Yes" or "No"

Show that every "No" has a value. You need an example of the value of a "No". A salesman is selling a product on which they make £50 profit per sale. Say that their conversion rate is 10%, which means that, for every ten potential customers they see, the salesman averages one sale. As they have to unlock nine "No" doors to reach the one marked "Yes", each "No" is worth £5 to the salesman.

I remember once explaining this to a direct salesman. 'Good heavens!' he said. 'If I knock on every door in Birmingham, I'll make a fortune!' I hadn't quite thought of it in that way but had to agree that the theory was sound.

He set out to do that and, every time a prospect said 'No', he replied, 'Thank you for your kind attention—and thank you for the £5 you have just earned me!' Not only did he find that this overcame his reluctance to door-knock, but he actually made a lot of extra sales from curious householders who said, 'Just a minute! How have I just earned you £5?' Once they started talking, a sale could follow, or, if not a sale, a referral.

And, yes, he did make a lot of money because he no longer took "Nos" personally and therefore found it easy to knock doors all day.

Get problems into perspective

A problem, when it first arises, can seem overwhelming. But a distributor can make it appear much more manageable just by changing their perspective on it. Here are some ways in which you can show them how to do that.

First, does the problem even exist?

Or is it only in their mind? Are they anticipating a problem which may never happen?

A famous businessman once asked me, 'Can you remember the problems you had this time last week?' Some—yes, I could remember easily. *But I had great difficulty in recalling the bulk of them.* He then went on to say, 'If you file all your problems in the waste-paper basket now, by this time next week, most of them will have either cured themselves or disappeared.' In other words, they either do not exist or they have been inflamed out of all proportion.

Has the distributor any other options for getting the income they want?

If the answer is "No", this is a classic case of turning a situation into a "must", and it may be enough to help them find the resolve necessary to overcome the problem.

Of course, if they have other options, these should be explored so that a distributor stops "sitting on the fence" and goes whole-heartedly for one option or the other. Even on a part-time basis, network marketing does not take kindly to half-hearted measures, so they must make up their mind: commit totally either to this business or to their other option.

Problems are simply part of life

Dream-creators understand this and accept that, in order to achieve any purpose, they will have to negotiate obstacles. The only trouble is that no one knows how many (page 39). What if the distributor you are working with were to give up just when the next obstacle would have been the last? Dream-creators are not prepared to take that risk, whereas dream-dumpers are.

One way to deal with this is to work out whether failing to deal with the problem will not lead to even worse problems. The problems of failure are usually worse than the problems of success, but few people can see that.

Are the distributor's purposes worth the effort required to overcome this obstacle?

The difference between success and failure is often nothing more than that one person can see quite clearly what success in overcoming that obstacle will bring, while another cannot.

Each time a distributor of yours meets a problem, get them to ask themselves, *'Are my ATAC Lifeplan and heart's desires worth the effort required to overcome this obstacle?'* In other words, get them to *Focus on their purposes* (Focus is one of the Six Winning Attitudes). It is amazing how often people, who are about to give in, suddenly find hidden reserves when they do this!

If you get a distributor you are working with to look at the problems they have successfully overcome in the past, they will see that they are no longer the looming obstacles they appeared to be at the time. This teaches them with the benefit of hindsight that:

A problem is not a barrier. It is only a temporary diversion on the road to success

---

Teaching a distributor to learn from hindsight makes it easier, when they meet future problems, to decide that these are only temporary diversions from the distributor's real heart's desires, and therefore worth the effort required to overcome them.

If a distributor knows with absolute certainty that they can overcome a problem, is it a problem any longer?

The point about obstacles is not that they exist but how important they are in a distributor's mind. If they can see a way *they feel comfortable with* to overcome an obstacle, they will do so and continue on their path towards their heart's desires. If they cannot see a solution *acceptable to themselves*, they will become dream-dumpers and drop out.

Overcoming a problem is only having the **Confidence** that they can do it, plus the **Knowledge** of how to overcome it. If they are not sure they can overcome it (and this is where you as a teacher can help), each obstacle is built up to be bigger than it actually is; they are seeing the obstacle as it was *before* they tackled it. Dream-creators, because they are totally confident they will overcome a problem (it is only a question of how), see it as smaller than it actually is because they are seeing it as if *after* it was overcome.

Part of your job as a teacher is to help distributors develop the confidence to overcome problems along the way, so that it is no longer a case of *if* a problem will be overcome but *how* and *when*. Seen in this way, you are helping them to reduce each problem to the point where they no longer see it as a barrier, but clearly as a temporary diversion.

Make the problem a common one, not peculiar to them

Help a distributor you are teaching to understand that the problem is a common one which is quite normal to other distributors, because it then becomes less of a threat. Problems which are seen by them as peculiar to themselves are usually the more dangerous to deal with.

Avoid comments like "When the going gets tough, the tough get going"

Comments like this may sound clever but they are not helpful. You might easily provoke the reaction: 'I don't think I'm tough enough, so I'd better get going!' They certainly do not make someone attempting to deal with a problem feel any better. In fact. They make problems seem more significant than they really are, when your job is to make them *less* significant and therefore easier to deal with.

Plan the route

Finally, if a distributor you are working with knows exactly where they are going and exactly what they have to do to get there, the problems they face will take on a less threatening aspect because they have become part of the route—deviations rather than barriers. This involves planning, so let's have a look at that next.

~ ~ ~

≈CHAPTER 16≈

People Who Fail To Plan, Plan To Fail

As a teacher, if you let the distributor you are working with take any Catherine wheel Actions, you are actually taking them away from their heart's desires, you have a prime responsibility to keep them in Rocket Action.

Your distributor's success comes not from action, but from *focused* or *directed* action

---

To help them plan their business, point them in the direction of *Target Success!*, which also has copies of all the relevant planning forms they will need for the whole of their first year. In this chapter, I will show you what is absolutely essential to cover with them.

How can you teach a distributor to be a rocket rather than a Catherine wheel? The first step is to get their agreement to:

The Six Planning Commitments
1. Will they make a commitment to what they want from the business?
2. Will they make a commitment to learning?
3. Will they commit to putting what they learn into practice?
4. Will they commit to doing a proper Contact List?
5. Will they make a commitment to your teaching strategy?
6. Will they make a commitment to their Business Activity Agreement?

---

1. Will they make a commitment to what they want from the business?

Where a distributor you are teaching is concerned, everything stems from what they want out of the business. And you can't do much as a teacher until you know what that is.

If the distributor you are working with is a high flyer, you should formalise their purposes on the ATAC Lifeplan, the Heart's Desires Card and the STARS Planning for Success Form (back page of *The Distributor's Action Plan*).

If they are less ambitious, the Planning for Success form may be enough for now, because often all they really want at this stage is to get their essential outgoings and replacement income covered.

The distributor you are working with will fall into one of four categories:

- They may only want to retail
- They may want to retail and business-build on a part-time basis
- They may be starting part-time with the intention of going full-time
- They may be aspiring to a high-level business.

Clearly, you will not teach someone who only wants to do a bit of retailing in the same way as you would someone who wants to build a high level business.

Commitments (2) and (3) are well covered elsewhere.

4. Will they commit to doing a proper Contact List?

The Contact List (Chapter 3, *The Secrets of Successful Recruiters*, Chapter 8, *Get Off To A Winning Start,* and *Target Success!*) is the foundation document for planning, which is why you should never work with anyone unless they have a proper one: i.e. a list with at least a hundred names. The only exception to this is if you are following the Peter Bloomfield system (page 163).

Should you help them make out their Contact List?

One view is that it is a waste of valuable time to help your new distributor draw up a Contact List. Another is that, given that it is so important, it is a good idea even though very time-consuming:

- It ensures that it is done. Is it better to spend a few hours helping someone with their list, or to see all the time you have invested in recruiting them wasted because they will not make one out?
- With your greater experience, you can help them dredge up more names, and make sure their Chicken List is included

- It increases the rapport between you and gets both of you into the habit of accompanying people in everything they do
- According to the Theory of Duplication, if you do this exercise with them, they are more likely to do the same with their people.

5. Will they make a commitment to your teaching strategy?

This means agreeing the plan for hitting their business targets on the Planning for Success Form.

Key to this is to accept that they must be accompanied in everything they do. Some distributors, particularly those from a business or sales background, can obstinately refuse to allow anyone to make phone calls with them, and insist on doing One-to-Ones. If so, there is no point in spending valuable time on them because, according to the Theory of Duplication, they will drag their group off-track and there's probably not a lot you can do about it.

The time a distributor you are teaching gives to network marketing needs to be **Quality Time.** If they have decided to allocate, for example, ten hours a week to the business, they can either waste that ten hours or, with your guidance, pack it with value. To do this, you need to make sure that both the **Content** and the **Attitude** are right.

Packing time with the right content

Teach the distributor you are working with to devote the whole of their allocated time purely and totally to four of the Eight Must-do Activities: retailing, recruiting, leading and teaching. The other four—developing the right attitudes (which include any learning activities such as the Thirty-Minutes-A-Day Habit), supporting events, targeting, and structuring their group—must be done in their own time. And, of course, all other activities that do not earn them money should be confined to "out of hours".

The right attitude to work

But the content of what people do is meaningless by itself. What brings it to life, what really packs value into the time they allocate to network marketing is to show them the importance of bringing both a sense of *Urgency in Action* and Enjoyment (part of being an ACTTER) to their business.

You may find that the distributor you are working with has never learnt to feel any urgency about work. But this is not a business for time-servers who just go through the motions. As for enjoyment, that is an emotion some have long since lost! If their mind has become conditioned to linking pain to work, due to years of doing a job from which they got no satisfaction, or suffering under bad management, you may have to teach them how to enjoy work again.

6. Will they make a commitment to their Business Activity Agreement?

The Business Activity Agreement or BACTA pulls together all the targets that experience shows your distributor should set themselves, and you will find a special form for it in *Target Success!*

What are the targets in the BACTA?
1. A retailing target
2. A personal contacting target
3. A downline contacting target
4. Their learning target
5. A BOM target
6. Their upline sizzle target
7. Their personal sizzle target
8. Their downline sizzle target
9. Their 2-2-2 target.

You will see that these are *Rocket Action* targets, aimed at helping you direct the distributor you are teaching very specifically towards hitting their business targets. But the BACTA can also act as their agreement of what they will do in return for your help. To get these targets to work best for you, you may need to amend them either generally, to fit in with the training system in your group, or individually, to suit the needs of the distributor you are working with.

The BACTA also fulfils two other functions. If your distributor writes down what they say they will do, they are much more likely to do it, and, just as important, they are less likely to deviate. It is easy to stray from a path if it cannot be seen. This is why so many workaholics and hard workers do not get the success their efforts deserve: they can deviate easily from the path because they haven't written it down. For this reason, you should always make sure that targets and the plans for achieving them are written down because it makes the distributor you are with much more likely to act.

When you are working with a distributor on their BACTA, make sure they understand that:

- The targets they set are their own, not yours. Remember that you should not dump your expectations onto your people
- They should constantly update their targets in line with the needs of their business or in response to changing conditions and advise you of these changes—so the BACTA will often need to be changed weekly
- To create regular, consistent work habits, try to agree with any distributor you are working with a regular time each week for discussing their next week's BACTA. The best days are usually Fridays, Saturdays or Sundays, in time to start the new week.

In comfort zone or out of comfort zone?

In terms of setting targets, the distributor you are working with will fall into one of two categories:

- They want to work outside their comfort zone
- They will not work outside their comfort zone.

Each requires entirely different teaching and leadership: if the distributor you are with belongs in the first group, they will drop out from frustration if you attempt to hold them back. If they belong in the second group, they will drop out if you push them too hard. So take this into account when you are helping them to set targets.

If they want to work outside their comfort zone, this is someone you really want because they could become one of your leaders! They want targets as high as possible. Your job is to make sure that, first, those targets are focusing their actions on achieving their purposes in the best possible way and, second, that they have paced themselves to last the marathon distance. If you let them sprint the first few laps and burn out (like Hyperactive Harold, page 102), you will have just lost that rare commodity, a natural hard worker.

If they do not want to work outside their comfort zone. These will be the great majority of your distributors. Present training systems tend to brand them as "drop out" material—*"People who are not prepared to pay the price"* is the expression often used. Trainers too often tell people that they must work outside their comfort zone and that, if they do not, they won't make it. Won't make what? Yes, this is true if someone wants to earn a high income, but many are satisfied with less.

Expect too much of people who will not work outside their comfort zones, and you will get nothing. Expect a little, and you will get something

---

We'll now go through each of the BACTA targets in turn.

1. Their retailing target

How much will they sell, depending on their circumstances, each week or each month? Remember the rules:

a. Everyone has to retail

b. How much each person retails is up to them

c. But everyone must set **at least** a monthly target and stick to it.

If the compensation plan of your company specifies a certain retail turnover to qualify for bonuses and royalties, that is the minimum retail target your distributors should set themselves. To hit that target, the number of people they will have to show the product to will depend on how good they are at retailing.

Retailing abilities vary enormously from one distributor to another, from those who can retail to almost anyone to those who can retail to almost no one. It may be that someone used to dealing with the general public in this way (a salesperson, a teacher, a receptionist and so on) may only have to show the product to two people to get a sale, whereas people who are not used to dealing with the general public (housewives who have been out of the job-market for years to bring up their children, manual workers or craftspeople, office-bound people from clerks to directors, or many professional people) may have to show the product to twenty people. That does not matter. If they both need to make two sales a week, the first person needs only to see four people; the other will need to see forty. But, if that is what they must do, they must do it.

2. Their personal contacting target

This is how many Get-Active calls they will make each day or each week.

The target is not how many contacts agree to a meeting, simply how many are phoned. Even if a contact refuses a meeting, the call will still count towards the target because we are just sorting the wheat from the chaff, those who want a look at the opportunity from those who do not.

If you are making these phone calls with them, the target must be at least 20 in an evening, or four to five 2-2-2s booked (*The Distributor's Action Plan*).

What about people who insist on making calls on their own?

Most teaching on making warm market phone calls consists of trying to get people to make more phone calls than they really want. But this is breaking the rule: *Don't dump your expectations onto your people.* The more you push, the more you set people up for stress and dream-dumping rather than pride in achievement, and the less you will get.

So do the complete opposite: encourage people to keep the target *down* to a level which you judge there is a good chance they really will achieve. This way, *A lot of people doing a little bit* will give you amazing results.

For example, say you have 100 distributors. Most group leaders would agree that about ten are doing most of the work so your problem is, how can I make the other 90 do something, no matter how little? How many calls a day are those 90 doing? We all agree, not many. But would they agree to making one a day? Yes, they'll all agree, but let's say 50 actually do. That will give you 1,500 calls a month. Are they making that number now?

Because of the stress and self-doubt involved, people often become inactive or drop out as a direct result of setting themselves targets they cannot keep to. Unless you as a teacher control this, the scenario you face with a new distributor might be something like this: on day one, they make twenty phone calls; seven on day two, five on day three...... By the end of the week, they have virtually stopped. Does this sound familiar? Did you do something like this? I did!

Here is another way to discuss the Personal Contacting Target:

> *'How many calls can you make a day?'*
>
> *'Oh, I think I can manage twenty'* [Or ten. Everyone thinks they can do a lot of calls, until they try!]
>
> *'Mmmm...... Shall we make that five calls a day? Let's just start with five until we see how you get on. We can always put it up later. Get into the habit of making five calls a day and your business will grow just fine. Tell you what, I'll give you a ring tomorrow to see how you got on.'*

Once they have set a target, decide from their Contact List who will be phoned today.

Tomorrow, phone them:

> *'How did you get on last night?'*
>
> *'I managed to make three phone calls.'*

Discuss those three and give advice. Then come back to:

> *'What was the problem with the other two?'*

Listen to the reason they give for not making them then, virtually whatever reasons they give, come back with:

> *'Are you going back to five calls tonight? Or, be honest, are you a little uncomfortable with making five?'*
>
> *'Well...... yes. To be honest, three was enough!'*
>
> *'No problem! Shall we drop your target for a while and see how you get on? Are you comfortable with three, or would two suit you better?'*
>
> *'No, no. Three was OK. I can do that.'*

The next secret is to follow up with the distributor you are working with *the day after* they make Get-Active calls. That way, you harness the power of Constant Repetition. Not only are you creating a habit—and people will not develop the contacting habit unless you consistently follow up the day after—but they will also, according to the Theory of Duplication, teach their people in the same way.

Following up promptly also means that you can nip problems in the bud and, if they are finding their target too difficult, you are in a position to suggest reducing it.

Of course, don't miss the opportunity of suggesting to a distributor that they increase their contacting target if they feel comfortable with doing so, in the light of their increasing confidence or motivation.

If a distributor will not agree to a BACTA, use a different strategy as shown on page 166.

3. Their downline contacting target

This is how many Get-Active phone calls the distributor you are working with will make with downlines that week. If you are working with a new distributor, this won't apply until they have a downline to work with.

4. Their learning target

This is the 30-Minutes-A-Day Habit, which breaks down to fifteen minutes of new study and fifteen minutes of recapping each day.

5. The BOM target (if your company promotes them)

How many BOMs will they attend each week? The minimum is one.

6. Their upline sizzle target

If there is an upline sizzle close enough, they should attend it. However, they should not attend more than one a week.

7. Their personal sizzle target

If you are working with a new distributor, this won't apply until they start their own sizzle sessions.

8. Their downline sizzle target

The purpose of this is to help downlines to hold better sizzles. If you are working with a new distributor, this won't apply until they have a downline who is holding sizzles.

9. Their 2-2-2 target

This is how many people the distributor you are working with will see each week, whether for themselves or a downline doesn't matter.

You may have noticed that distributors are not asked to set themselves a target for the number of hours they are prepared to devote each week to building their businesses. This is not an essential target because the number of hours worked is less important than what is done in those hours. All the targets in the BACTA relate to productivity because it is productivity you want. But there is no reason why you cannot add that target if you so wish, either generally or in cases where you think it might be relevant.

The distributor you are with should now plan the BACTA activities into a weekly diary.

Finally, get them to fill in a single sheet Monthly Planner (see *Target Success!*). This is not used for specific appointments: it is too small for that. The idea is to give both you, as the teacher, and the distributor you are teaching a balanced monthly overview of their level of activity under the headings of:

- Strategy Meetings
- Retailing Visits
- Contacting Calls
- 2-2-2s
- BOMs/Sizzles/Trainings.

The Monthly Planner also gives them an incentive to fill up the month ahead with productive work!

The key to achieving targets is Consistency

There are other really effective, business-building ways to plan and target work. For these, see *Target Success!* But setting proper targets is only half the battle; if you want to help the distributor you are working with to reach them, you should also explain the importance and the meaning of **Consistency.** In other words, they must carry out each of the Eight Must-do Activities consistently every day, every week or every month depending on the requirements of each target.

Watch out for Hyperactive Harold!

Hyperactive Harold tells you he will put in ten hours a week, and then puts in ten hours a day. He goes off like a rocket, lighting up the sky with a shower of sparks. He forgets to take his mother-in-law to Bingo, his wife only sees him when he needs a clean shirt, his children ask, 'Mummy, mummy—who's that strange man?' and his boss gets angry at the amount of unfinished work on Hyperactive Harold's desk.

But you think, 'Great! Hyperactive Harold is really taking off! He's going to be a real benefit to my business!'

Except for one thing: six weeks later, Hyperactive Harold falls out of your business. His mother-in-law has hit him with a rolling pin, his wife has threatened divorce, he suddenly realises how much he is missing his children and his boss has sent him a warning letter.

Hyperactive Harold's sponsor did himself no favours by not advising him to hold back and stick to his BACTA!

Now, give your commitment to them

Explain that this is their business but, if they give you these Six Commitments, you will help them to build it. But you will only build it *with* them, not *instead of* them. In other words, your commitment to them is to match your efforts to theirs. If they go all-out to hit their BACTA targets, so will you. But if they are half-hearted then you will not put yourself out.

~ ~ ~

≈CHAPTER 17≈

More Tips For Winning Teachers

What separates a winning teacher from an ordinary one is often only that they come across better to people. So to complete Part II on Winning Teaching I'll give you some useful tips on how to do this by being a better Leaders' ACTTER.

Assume new distributors know nothing

It can be demoralising for a distributor you are teaching if you assume that they know something when they do not. People do not like to admit ignorance and, worse, you will make them feel inadequate.

How much did you know when you started? We can all too easily forget that there was a time when we knew nothing about the business, either! Always try to remember what it was like for you when you started, and you won't go far wrong.

So, until you know how much someone you are working with knows, assume that it is up to you to show them everything.

Some of your distributors may have more conventional business experience than you. Some may have reached the top of their previous careers. Don't be overawed by this; they may have been the experts in their old occupation but you are the expert in this one—and don't be afraid to say so if it becomes necessary. No matter how much knowledge they have of other things, unless they have been in network marketing before, they will know nothing about this industry.

Treat a distributor you are working with as if they are going to "make it"

A run of drop-outs or people who sign up and insist, despite your every effort, on "doing their own thing" and going off track, can sometimes make you cynical, especially towards new distributors.

If you allow yourself to feel resigned to "going through the motions" with a distributor, this will communicate itself subconsciously to them. If their sixth sense tells them that you think they will drop out or that they are unteachable, they are half-way to just that! Remember that you cannot tell who will or who will not succeed. What you can do is to increase their chances of failure—by your negative attitude.

Treat every communication with a distributor as a teaching opportunity

This business is unusual in that, every time you are teaching a distributor, whether face-to-face, by phone or in writing, you are also showing them how to teach their people.

According to the Theory of Duplication your distributors will, whether you like it or not, copy the way you handle any given situation. If they are going to copy you anyway, it is surely better that you give them good habits to copy, rather than bad ones!

So, before you deal with any particular situation, ask yourself:

> *'Is the way I am about to tackle this the way I would want it to cascade down my network?'*

A good habit is to take every opportunity to remind a distributor you are working with that *Every communication is also a teaching opportunity;* before every meeting or at the start of each phone call, say something like, "Remember that what we discuss today, you may want to cover at some point with one of your distributors" or, "Everything you learn today, you must pass onto your distributors" or, "You may need to handle this problem sometime in the future, so treat this as a teaching session in how to deal with it".

Some top network marketeers even make the 2-2-2 a teaching session, not only for the distributor who is accompanying them, *but for the person they are showing the business to as well!* They say to the prospect, 'This meeting could also be your first training session because, if you *do* like what you hear today and decide to come into this business, the way I show you the business will be the best way for you to show the business to *your* prospects. Of course, if you decide that the business is not for you, that will not apply.'

Don't teach how you would do it, teach the best way for your new distributor to do it

We are all different and different people will do the same job in different ways depending on their talents, skills, character, background and experience.

An obvious example is how people say things. A distributor's choice of words should be what sounds natural coming from them, not what may sound right coming from you. This is particularly important when you are helping them to prepare suitable scripts for the Get-Active phone calls or for dealing with objections.

The same is true of the 2-2-2. You may be much more articulate than the distributor you are teaching—or they may be much more articulate then you; and perhaps one of you has a much quieter personality than the other, or one is humorous and the other serious. The result is that, although the structure or framework of the 2-2-2 should not change, you will present yourselves differently within it.

It is very easy to assume that, because a distributor is doing something differently from the way you would, they must be doing it wrongly. The way to avoid this is to, before you speak, ask yourself, *Will what I am about to say or do actually make them:*

- Faster
- Or more efficient
- Or more effective?

If it does none of those things, leave well alone!

Don't point out a problem until you know the answer

There are few things more destructive than saying to someone you are working with that they have a problem—but you don't know what to do about it!

Until you told them, they were very possibly unaware that they had a problem so, as far as they are concerned, there wasn't one until you mentioned it! But, by bringing it to their attention without a solution, you have definitely created a problem and, because you have no solution, you will have done an excellent job of undermining their confidence.

If you do not know the solution to a problem, keep quiet about it until you have had a chance to work one out or discuss it with an upline.

Think before you speak

Not only does this avoid the problem we have just discussed, it is always best to think out the simplest and most effective way to present your point before you do so. This is all part of KISSing and playing CUPID. Remember what we said before: *The way you teach them will be the way they teach their people* (the Theory of Duplication), and you want the simplest way passed on.

Raise problems in a positive way

Try to avoid phrases like "You did that wrong" or, "That was a mistake". It is better to say something like, "Next time you try that, why not have a go at doing it this way?" or, "Would it improve it if you did that?" or, "Is it worth a go at trying this?"

Showing someone how to do something better is usually more effective than showing them how to stop doing it badly, although there are times when the only way you can get through to them is by doing the latter. If they simply won't listen you may, as a last resort, have to try shock tactics: 'Unless you stop doing that, you are going to have a serious problem with the business!'

Limit criticism and balance with praise

A winning teacher you should always be looking for the areas in which you can help a distributor improve; not at what they are already doing well. This can make it very easy to start coming out with a catalogue of criticisms or "areas for improvement".

This is a great way to make someone who is actually doing an excellent job believe that they are totally incompetent! It is common for managers in traditional business to use the tactic of constant criticism as a way of keeping their staff in a subservient position. Fortunately, this has no place in network marketing. Having said that, it is very easy to undermine someone's confidence by mistake! So how do you prevent that from happening?

1. Limit the teaching topics

Choose only a very few topics at a time on which to teach. Remember *Confuse to lose*? If there is a topic that needs a lot of work done on it and which is holding a distributor back, you might decide to deal with that on its own.

Which are the best topics to choose? Those most getting in the way of a distributor's success. You may find The Pyramid to Success (page 41) helpful in deciding this.

2. Get the basics right first

You should help a distributor to do a competent overall job—getting the "broad brush strokes" in—before becoming involved in nitty-gritty detail work which will only ever result in small, marginal improvements.

Because these tend to be big topics, make sure you break them into bite-sized chunks first, so that your new distributor can experience success in tangible, small steps, and second, so that you do not overwhelm them with detail.

You will notice that I applied this rule to *The Secrets Series* and The STARS Leadership Programme:

1. I start new distributors off with *The Secrets Series*. This makes learning very simple, using broad brush strokes to give them a broad overview of what they have to do, just enough to get their businesses started

2. In *Get Off To A Winning Start*, I use a slightly finer brush, dealing with the start-up period in more detail, but still nothing very difficult—and certainly nothing anyone cannot do

3. In *Breakthrough Recruiting & Retailing* I used a medium brush, introducing broad-based concepts like the ACTTER, KISS and CUPID, and so on

4. Now in this book, we are down to the fine brush work, painting in all the details.

Can you imagine what would happen if you started a new distributor on this book? They would be overwhelmed. But, having worked through *The Secrets Series* and the earlier titles of The STARS Leadership Programme, and also by now having had some experience, I don't suppose there is anything here that is "blowing your mind".

3. Balance with praise

If someone you are teaching is keen to succeed and willing to learn, you can always assume that they are doing the best job of which they are currently capable. It may seem to you that they are terrible, but remember that their *only* agreement with you is this: provided that they are on the On-Track Path, you *will* help them to achieve the standards they will need to succeed.

Part of being a Leaders' **A**CTTER is that you are **A**ccountable to people to help them succeed. There is nothing there about how good they have to be by any given time! So, as well as giving them the **R**espect (also part of being a Leaders' ACTTE**R**) they deserve for doing the best they can, *you must make them feel good about something*. Tell them what they are doing best.

This is where Patience, one of the Six Winning Attitudes, pays off. Handled in the right way, some of your people who start out the worst can often turn out to be the best. But they definitely will not if you show impatience and don't nurture them properly!

Show respect for their sphere of influence

Everyone likes to feel that the boundaries of their territory are being **R**espected (part of being a Leaders' ACTTE**R**). Even if you are teaching a new distributor, they are still the "managing director" of their own business; so confirm their status as the head of their group when you are in the presence of their distributors or prospects.

Some of us have massive egos but this is the time to lock them away! If you are attending a distributor's sizzle, a BOM or a training run by them, try not to take over, difficult though that sometimes is! Defer to them, make it clear that they are the "boss" for the occasion. Ask them what they would like you to do, then stick to it. Whether you feel it or not, show them the respect they deserve for being the leader of their group.

If you do not do this, if you tend to "take over", your distributors will not want you at their meetings and you will undermine their people's confidence in their leader. But if you do treat them with respect, if you respect their sphere of influence, you will build great loyalty, you will always be welcome and, most important of all, you will have helped to confirm the confidence of their people in them as a group leader.

Be consistent in your behaviour

Teachers who show mood-swings or who keep changing policies depending on what they heard yesterday are very unsettling, especially to a new distributor! A distributor you are teaching will learn much more quickly and develop greater confidence in you, if you get them into an established pattern and routine and if they get used to you always being a Leaders' ACTTER.

Be an example of what you are teaching: set high standards for yourself

---
This is a professional business. Your standards are your group's standards

---

So you should look and be professional in the way you talk, act, prepare and carry out the business. You should develop a sense of urgency and, where meetings are concerned, the attitude *First to arrive, last to leave* is a great example.

Although there are far fewer rules and procedures laid down by the company in network marketing than in traditional business, there still are rules and procedures so it is important that you give an example by following them.

This, of course, means that you must *Practise what you preach.* Unlike in conventional business, *Do what I say, not what I do* does not work because, according to the Theory of Duplication, you will be teaching your people to do the same thing when they start teaching.

Before a 2-2-2, decide who does what, and stick to it

This means <u>C</u>larify the agenda (part of playing <u>C</u>UPID).

Before you start any teaching or accompanied session, and this includes a 2-2-2, agree what is going to happen. Distributors learn much more quickly if they have an agenda to follow.

The best way for new distributors to LEARN is to DO

People learn much more from *doing* than they do from *listening*. This is why accompanying someone in everything they do is so much more effective than Arm's Length training.

Yes, it is quicker to do things yourself in the short-term, but the more you make a new distributor do, the quicker they will learn and the sooner you can move on to another new distributor.

So you need to resist the temptation to do too much yourself just because you lack the Patience (a Winning Attitude) to explain what you want done. Ego can also make you want to do things yourself, rather than letting someone else do it. So can boredom—it is much more interesting to do it yourself than to have to watch someone else for the thousandth time! A good way to keep yourself alert and not be tempted to interrupt through boredom is to take notes which you can use in the discussion with your distributor after the 2-2-2.

However, be careful not to go too far in giving a new person things to do. If you make people do things before their confidence or competence levels are ready for them, it will be detrimental and will mean that you actually have to spend more time with them before they are ready to take over. It is all a question of balance, common sense and sensitivity to how they are coping.

As a teacher, it can be very tempting to take over the 2-2-2. Not only might distributors find this infuriating but, unless you let them do as much as possible as quickly as possible, they are not going to learn and you will be encouraging the problem of Dependency.

The hardest time to hold yourself back is when you can see it going wrong for a distributor in a 2-2-2. The argument is that, unless you intervene to rescue the situation, there is no chance of recruiting that prospect. Apart from that, you would be pretty hard-hearted if sympathy did not make you want to step in to save your distributor from further embarrassment.

But taking over the 2-2-2 is not the way to handle this situation:
- The best way for your distributors to learn how to get out of situations is to get into them in the first place! If they don't handle it well, you can show them a better way afterwards. It is better to lose one prospect now than, perhaps, many later
- You are, again, encouraging Dependency if your distributors realise that you will step in to save them.

Admit your mistakes—and laugh at them!

By laughing at your mistakes you show that you **E**njoy the business (part of being a Leaders' ACTT**E**R) and are having fun!

Some managers subscribe to the theory that people lose confidence in leaders who make mistakes. The complete opposite is the case. Potentially big business-builders come into network marketing because they (correctly) believe that *anyone* can reach the top; if they stop believing in that possibility, they will drop out. Your distributors must be able to feel that they can do what you do, but who believes they can copy perfection?

New distributors are often frightened of making mistakes, particularly if they have come from a big organisation where the very worst crime is to make a mistake (the second worst is to admit to it). This can hold back their willingness to just get out and have a go! If they see you in your teaching capacity treating mistakes lightly, can you imagine how this lifts a load off their shoulders?

People who are not frightened of making mistakes or of making fools of themselves learn very much more quickly than those who are. Until you can take the risk of looking foolish, you will never release your full potential. The same is true of someone you are teaching.

The real failure is not in making a mistake, it is in not "having a go". Those who are not prepared to make mistakes never achieve anything

---

The only people who do not make mistakes are the dead!

Leave them with Self-Training Aims

Self-training is one of the most productive tools in a teacher's armoury, yet in network marketing it is hardly ever used.

After an on-the-job session, and as the last thing you do before you leave, discuss with the distributor you are working with what the best subject for self-training would be. The reason you leave this until last is because that is what will stay in the distributor's mind, and therefore there is more chance that it will get done.

This is such a successful technique because it requires the distributor to focus for a period on a particular topic chosen by you. Any subject can be chosen for this treatment: any part of their phone call or 2-2-2 technique, any aspect of the way in which a distributor teaches their people or handles contacts at BOMs, the way they run sizzle sessions, public speaking at meetings and Formal Trainings— or anything else you can think of.

Some bad habits can be extremely difficult to break and some good ones difficult to acquire, and these can respond well to an intensive period of self-training.

For most people, self-training aims are an essential apart of developing the right attitude; indeed, it is difficult to think of any other way of doing this which is as quick and effective. Changing attitudes takes us into the realms of personal development and, if you think about it:

Just about every book and training on personal development is seeking to get you to set self-training aims

---

Once a self-training aim is agreed, you should advise the distributor of the best materials (books, tapes, CDs and videos) available to deal with that topic. However, there are plenty of bad materials around, and you should make a point of finding out which ones will do your distributors more harm than good. At the very least, harm is done by the wasted cost of buying them and the waste of time in studying them. At the worst, bad materials drag them off track.

It is one thing to agree a self-training aim with a distributor, it is quite another to get them to do it! In many cases, they will not deliberately omit to carry out self-training aims; these can get forgotten in the midst of all the other things they have to do. This can especially be the case when you are teaching a new distributor, who will not yet have acquired good work habits.

So use Constant Repetition: *Every time you speak to them*, whether personally or by phone, ask how they are getting on with their self-training aim. Once they realise that this is going to be discussed at every opportunity, they will soon develop the habit of carrying out whatever activity has been agreed!

Once the purpose of the current self-training aim has been achieved, a new one should be agreed.

Set yourself Self-Training Aims

As a teacher and leader responsible for helping others to succeed, it is even more important that you seek to keep developing yourself. As you develop, you will find that your self-training aims incline more towards personal development rather than being directly job-related.

Theory versus practice

As I said on page 70, there is going to be a difference between how much time you *ought* to spend with a new distributor (i.e., until he or she knows as much as you do), and how much time you *can* spend with them, given the demands on your time as more and more people need your support.

So I'll give you a four-point plan to deal with this:

1. Start them on *The Secrets Series* and then follow up with The STARS Leadership Programme
2. Keep in frequent phone contact, talking through techniques
3. Keep their self-training aims going
4. Make discussions on how to teach and lead an important part of sizzles and other meetings. Hold regular seminars on these topics—monthly if you can get at least five people attending.

In this way, and only in this way, will you get distributors to mature into expert, professional teachers and leaders within three to six months of joining.

Effective teaching should lead to enjoyable action!

Now that we are reaching the end of Part II, *Be A Winning Teacher!*, I want to leave you with three thoughts:

First, your tuition should not replace the attitude of *Urgency in Action*. Its *sole* purpose is to help someone you are working with to *do* better.

Second, there is a danger that tuition can take the spontaneity and fun out of a job. It shouldn't. Proper tuition should bring more fun as well as success.

Third, never let your teaching get in the way of a distributor just getting on with it. Teaching should lead to more Rocket Action, not less, more enthusiasm and Focus, not less, and a Bulldozer Mentality. And never let the technique become more important than the results.

Although we have covered a lot of detail, I hope you did not find anything particularly difficult. Anyway, don't worry too much about the detail at this stage. Once you start to practise the craft of being a winning teacher, you will find that everything will soon slot into place. The main thing is to keep reading and rereading this section and comparing it with what you are actually doing with your people.

Very soon, it will all be automatic.

Now we go on to the final part of the book, Part III, where we explore the art of winning leadership.

~ ~ ~

Part III

Be A Winning Leader!

Although everyone becomes a leader whether they like it or not the minute they recruit their first distributor, we have seen that there are two distinct types of leader. If you are a small to medium-sized business-builder, you may prefer to delegate the leadership of your group to the upline distributors who have chosen to take on active leadership roles. You do this through applying the Figure-of-Eight Attitude, connecting your downlines with your uplines.

*You may, of course, want to take on a more prominent or what we call **active** leadership role. Indeed, if you want a high income or a large group, you will have to. The final section of this book is written primarily for those who want to become active leaders.*

But even if you are not taking on an active leadership role at this stage of your business, you will find great benefit in reading this section for three reasons:

1. *For running your own group*
2. *You will be more help to your upline active leaders if you understand what their job entails*
3. *You will know how to direct the efforts of any downliners who are serious about building a big group.*

≈CHAPTER 18≈

As A Leader, How Do You Get The Best Out Of Your Group?

In this chapter, we will take a look at what being a winning leader means, in other words, how you get the best out of your people.

In Chapter 4 we saw that, although your people are all self-employed, the great majority want to be part of a structure and a team. The more experienced network marketing leaders become, the more you will see them behaving like the leaders of conventional businesses. In other words, they create a recognised and acceptable way of doing things for their group, and they expect their distributors to follow that path.

Where you will differ from the leaders of conventional business is the way in which you should handle those who do not conform. A conventional leader uses disciplinary actions; in the final analysis these could be dismissal or termination of contract. You, as a network marketing leader, having discharged the responsibility of showing a distributor the right way of doing things and warning them of what might happen if they go off track, let them go their own way. One of three things will happen to those of your group who choose to do that:

- They will fail and drop out
- They will realise the error of their ways and come back to the fold
- By some miracle, they will succeed.

Only in the second case will you, the upline, come back into the equation (although in the third eventuality you will be in the nice position of receiving royalties for doing nothing!)

Be a leader, not a manager! Lead on your feet, not from your butt! Lead from the front!

Managers are the bane of British business. They think they are leaders but they are not; they sit behind desks telling other people what to do but are not prepared to do it themselves. They no longer believe that they must give a good example to their people. They will not lower themselves to "rolling their sleeves up and getting stuck in". Their motto is *Do what I say, not what I do.*

Winning leaders are the complete opposite. They lead from the front. They lead by example. They "muck in", "roll their sleeves up" and work with their people on the job. They are always to be seen in the thick of what is going on. They gain the respect of their group because they are seen to share their tribulations with them.

A winning leader has broad shoulders and a small butt, a manager has small shoulders and a big butt. A winning leader looks to the front, a manager looks over their shoulder. There is no room for managers in network marketing—only for leaders

---

If you want to be a winning leader, spend as much time as you can out there with your group, showing them by example how to accompany their people in everything they do, be seen at meetings, trainings, sizzles and BOMs, and mix with them as much as you can.

If you lead from the front, your group will follow you. If you lead from behind, your group will hang back with you.

Take responsibility!

Again, don't imitate the managers of conventional business. To them, "taking responsibility" means, "I am responsible for any success but you are responsible for any failure"! Is anyone else except you going to make your group successful? No? Then you might as well accept total responsibility for making your success happen.

A winning leader does not worry about how much ability they have

---

Your group needs your *support*, not your *talent*. The support you give your group will overcome any lack of talent you think you might have

---

Actually, if you understand this, you have the one talent that really matters because you understand what the Keystone Law really means—that if you give your group the framework and the environment they need to succeed, *you* will succeed. There are many so-called talented people out there who do not build the size of group they want because they do not understand that:

Your abilities cannot make up for any lack of results in your group, but your group can make up for any apparent lack of ability in you

---

…… if you give them the leadership they need.

If, as a winning leader in network marketing, you do not need to do the job better than your people, what abilities do you need? Exactly the same as those of a captain, not of a ship, who needs a different type of relationship with their crew, but of a sports team, albeit a very large one! What do the players on a team want of their captain?:

How To Be The Captain Of Your Group

- No one in the team expects the captain to do a better job than they do, but they do expect the captain to have a better *attitude* to the job than they do, which means that, although the captain cannot do the job better than they can, the captain tries harder than they do, trains harder, works harder, is more committed to success than they are, and is more competitive than they are
- They do not expect the captain to do a better job than they do but they do want the captain to help them be better at what they do
- They expect the captain to *know* more about the job than they do, even if the captain cannot *do* it better
- They expect the captain to be loyal to them and to support them when they need it
- They expect the captain to listen to what they say but then, having made a decision, have the courage to stick to it, no matter how unpopular it is. But they also expect the captain to do what is best for the team, which means having the wisdom to change that decision if it becomes clear that it is the wrong one
- They expect the captain to lead from the front. If the captain leads from the front, the team will follow; if the captain does not, the players will hang back with the captain. So they want the captain to show them the way, to lay down the ground rules, not to be better than the players at what they do
- What gains the team's respect is the willingness of the captain to get onto the playing field with them, to be in the thick of the game with them, to share their triumphs and disappointments, not to be better than they are.

You need exactly the same attributes as the captain of that team. It is being seen to be doing and sharing that are important, not how well you do it.

As a leader, how tough do you need to be?

Many people opt out of leadership because they believe it means having to be tough and uncaring, and they would rather be more "human". But this doesn't follow. Being a winning leader is not the same as "riding roughshod" over people.

Toughness should only mean being a straight, honest talker and *Urgent in Action*, prepared to tell a group what it is in their own interests to do in order for them to get results. If it goes beyond this into using rather than helping people, it is unacceptable.

Caring means understanding people so that you know how best to motivate them to get the results they want. It is not sympathising with people who are not doing their best, or sidestepping unpleasant but necessary actions, or keeping quiet about unpalatable truths that people need to know for their own sakes. That is merely weakness.

True responsibility means being tough when you need to be, caring when you need to be, and knowing the difference

---

Therefore, true caring often means having to be tough. The over-caring person may lose fewer people because of their management style, but they are not good at getting the best out of them. Tough-but-caring leaders, although they may sometimes go too far and lose distributors, will always do better overall because they are good at helping people to stretch themselves.

There are two sorts of leader: those who think the group is there for their benefit, and those who think they are there for the group's benefit

---

You and your group will, I am sure, know all about managers in conventional organisations who think that the organisation is there for their benefit. They do ride roughshod over people. They are not interested in finding out what is best for the organisation, only what is best for themselves; the result is that they do not listen to their staff and they try to impose their views on people, instead of finding out the best way to get the job done.

I'm not saying that this is not how some big business-builders in network marketing lead their groups, but I will show you a better and easier way. If you want to apply the Keystone Law (which means that getting the best out of your group is what is best for you), see yourself as the opposite of these managers like this—as being there *for the benefit of the group*—to serve. Your decision-making will then be entirely different: instead of deciding for yourself what the right decision is and then imposing it, you will listen very openly to the group's views before making up your mind.

Where the toughness comes in is that:

- If distributors are pre-disposing themselves to failure unless they are on the On-Track Path, you must be tough enough not to waste your time with anyone who chooses a different route, and firm enough to ensure that your leaders and teachers do the same

- You must be tough enough to listen carefully and with an open mind *even to people you think are wrong*. Listen to everybody. Very often, it is the newest people with a fresh point of view who will notice the flaws that everyone else has become blind to, or who see the creative solution which experienced people miss because it is outside the accepted way of doing things. Also, people who do not agree with your final decision will accept it much more readily if they feel that you gave them a fair chance to put their point of view

- You must be tough enough, once a decision is made, to make sure it is carried out

- If the decision does not get the results expected, you must be tough enough to reopen the debate and, if necessary, admit you were mistaken and change your opinion.

Sticking with a course of action that is obviously not going to work is not tough, it is stupid—or weak because you cannot admit that you were wrong. It takes a tough person, but a person genuinely working for the good of the group, to say, 'My decision did not work, it is time to find another solution.'

The great thing about network marketing is that you can actually look around and see effective leaders in action. You will notice that people who are committed to succeeding will gravitate towards those leaders who are straight-talking; they want leaders who will <u>T</u>ell *it as it is* (part of being a Leaders' AC<u>T</u>TER).

You will also see group leaders who are so anxious to be liked that they find it impossible to be straight and honest with their group. They are not prepared to accept the harsher realities of following the On-Track Path, and they let their group believe that other ways to success are just effective. This makes them responsible for the failure of people who trusted them to give the right guidance. With this in mind, weak leaders are no better than callous ones because each causes equal damage to their people.

Yes, you do need to be tough if that means:

✓ Being caring enough about your group to be straight and honest with them

✓ Being responsible enough to find out what is actually needed for success—not what you hope, would like or prefer to be needed—and

✓ Being dedicated enough to pass this onto your group.

Your job as a leader is to light the *right* way

Accept that wonderful and privileged responsibility, and you will be not just a winning leader but a great leader, deserving of the respect, the loyalty and, above all, the success that you will get.

Earlier, I said that the definition of Winning Leadership is:

Training + Direction + Motivation

A winning leader is good at all three, so we will now look at each of them in turn, starting with training.

~ ~ ~

≈CHAPTER 19≈

How To Have The Best Trainings On The Block

**Winning Leadership =
TRAINING + Direction + Motivation**

We have looked in detail at teaching as seen through your eyes as a winning *teacher*. As a winning *leader*, there is a wider aspect to training: how you get your training methods and standards through to the group as a whole, rather than, as in your function as a teacher, concentrating on individual group members.

There is not usually any shortage of Arm's Length trainings going on in groups. But as a winning leader, your aim will be to ensure that these are used only to support people being accompanied in everything they do not, as is normally the case, instead of it. You will also want to ensure that your group are ACTTERS who KISS and play CUPID, and that in addition in their teaching role, they are Leaders' ACTTERs and they follow the Steps of Training.

It is one thing to attain high standards and check that only good teaching habits are being practised when your group is small. It is quite another to keep them that way when the group gets large or during periods of fast growth in your distributor base.

When a leader achieves the level of income and the lifestyle they have been working for, a new danger threatens—**Inertia.** When you are earning what you want, it becomes even easier to slip into a comfort zone, and with this comes falling standards, bad habits and people talking a good act instead of doing a good job.

You have two ways of avoiding this:
1. Constant Repetition of the lessons of network marketing
2. Making sure that you and your leaders constantly lead from the front, lead by example and focus on seeing that their people are accompanied in everything they do.

Part II, *Be A Winning Teacher!*, concentrated mainly on accompanying people in everything they do because that is the primary function of a winning teacher. However, Arm's Length training does have an extremely important part to play in its own right and we covered this on page 35. Let's now take a closer look at what is involved.

The two forms of Arm's Length training

- *Formal Training,* also called classroom training, where the training is presented in a formal way
- *Reactive Training,* where the trainer reacts to the specific needs or problems of an individual or group. Training over the phone and the confusingly named "one-to-one" meetings with a distributor (as opposed to 2-2-2s with a prospect) are mostly of a reactive nature. Sizzle sessions are also an important part of Reactive Training and we will cover these in the next chapter.

Formal Trainings can be called "nuts and bolts" trainings to differentiate them from motivational meetings. Whether formal training or motivational meeting, they are often referred to as **seminars,** and can take place in a variety of formats: one hour, two hours, one day, two days, evenings, week-ends. You can also have regular weekly or monthly seminars or occasional "one-off" meetings. They are often run before or after BOMs, but this can get in the way of guests being properly looked after at the BOM—and it is not always the right tactic to have guests sitting in on a training.

Some leaders like to "keep their group to themselves"

These are the "lone wolves" we looked at on page 22. They discourage their people from co-operating with other groups and encourage group insularity. If you want to be as successful a dream-creator as you can be, theirs are not the ranks to join.

Do you need to organise your own group BOMs, trainings and events to be a winning leader?

For ease of reference, we will lump together BOMs, trainings and other meetings as "events".

Please note that we are not including sizzle sessions as an event because, once their group starts to build, every distributor looking for a reasonable sized group should be running their own "closed" meetings or sizzle sessions (that is, restricted to invited downlines). We will have a look at these in the next chapter.

In the early stages, you do not need to set up your own events. In fact you should not if there are other *good* events in the geographical areas where your group is active, because you can link yourself and your group into those.

Once a group reaches a certain size, its leaders may want to look at setting up their own group events. If other good events are available it is not essential, although there probably is a benefit if you intend to become a big business-builder.

Before you decide whether to organise your own events, there are some points to bear in mind:

- One of the great things about network marketing is that distributors co-operate in helping each other to build their businesses, *even if they are in different groups in the network.*

Good teamwork does not just apply upline and downline, it applies crossline and into other groups as well.

Any action that turns co-operation between distributors or groups into competition is simply unacceptable

- Events need to be of a certain size before they can generate the **group dynamic** or **group momentum** so essential to their success. Therefore, it is far better if local distributors from all groups in a given geographic area co-operate on one event until the attendance is big enough to support another. So it is not acceptable to set up an event in an area if, by doing this, you will make an existing one unsustainable. When the other local event is big enough to create its own group momentum without the people you will draw away from it, then it is perfectly acceptable to start your own

- If other events in the area are not of a high standard, as a winning leader you must either offer to help improve them or start your own. Inactivity is not an option—there is no such thing as a winning leader with a badly trained or motivated group!
- There is no point in organising a worse event than another one available in the area. That is vanity! Yours must be at least as good as, if not better than, *all* others in the area. If it is not, swallow your pride, close down your event and tie in with the best one around
- Just as your people should be welcomed at events held by other groups, so distributors from other groups and, if relevant, their guests must be made welcome at yours.

What if you are a bad public speaker?

There is no such thing—there are only badly *trained* public speakers. *Anyone* can learn to become a competent speaker at events.

There are two sorts of speaker needed:

- ***Trainers who play KISS and play CUPID,*** presenting training simply and logically, so that their audience can learn in the easiest possible way
- ***Motivators.*** More ability is required to be a good motivational speaker, but if a person is prepared to speak from the heart with Pride (one of the Six Winning Attitudes) and can learn to love their audience, they can acquire the skill. This may not make them a great motivational speaker, but they can, nevertheless, make people feel good about themselves—and that is what counts.

In any case, the point is not whether you could become a good public speaker but whether you would enjoy speaking week-in, week-out at events. If not, don't do more than you must to be seen to be leading from the front! There will be plenty of other distributors who are willing to speak. You organise, you decide the course content and, in the main, they speak. It is a good tactic to invite speakers from other groups within the network because the more that different groups co-operate at local level, the more each will benefit.

The important thing is to control the quality of what is going on—in this case, making sure that your group members have the best possible trainings for themselves, the best possible BOMs to take their guests to and the most motivating events possible.

How to make your events as effective as possible

Remember who they are for!

Events should only be held if they will benefit your *distributors* although, in some cases such as BOMs, this actually means that the interests of their *guests* should come first. Events are not showcases for your vanity or for the egos of your group leaders or speakers:

Plan the whole event and the course content to answer the needs of your distributors or guests, not to cater for the egos of you and your group leaders.

At every event, the least experienced, least talented, least confident slowest learners are the people who matter most

This is supposed to be a simple business. Speakers who do not ensure that the least experienced, least talented, least confident slowest learners have understood are not KISSing and playing CUPID, and they have already started to complicate things.

Therefore, make sure that all content is aimed at helping people in this category to understand it.

Use a variety of speakers

If the event is one at which guests are present, having speakers from both sexes and from a variety of ages and backgrounds helps to ensure that if a guest does not relate to one speaker, they may warm to another. It also proves what they have been told: that dream-creators come from all sorts of background.

Variety of speakers at a training boosts the confidence of your group because it shows them in action that successful network marketeers do, indeed, come from every background. But it also serves another purpose: trainings generally involve a lot of content, and there is only so much the listeners can take in. For them, a variety of speakers helps to maintain interest and concentration—a change is as good as a rest.

However, do not delay an event just because you cannot get enough speakers of an adequate standard. Remember that events should be held for the benefit of your people; if it is more valuable for them to have a session held by one speaker than to have no session at all, then hold it.

The only other exception to the rule of variety is when you invite an outside expert, well-known personality or great motivational speaker to talk to your people.

Make sure your speakers KISS and Play CUPID

In the introduction to every event, remember **C**—**C**larify *the agenda*. It takes a great deal away if people are not absolutely clear in their own minds about what is going on.

Many distributors and guests, possibly the majority, do not come from good educational backgrounds. They, and their needs, must be respected. Some topics are not easy to explain, but that is no excuse for speakers making them even more difficult by not KISSing and playing CUPID.

If a seminar is going to last for several hours—and most will—the simpler your speakers make the content, the more will be remembered when those who attended go back to whichever of their up-lines is accompanying them in everything they do.

Avoid questions!

It will often be necessary to use inexperienced distributors as speakers, and BOMs are regularly used to give people their first taste of public speaking. So can I suggest you do not allow questions unless *all* the speakers can handle them (it is no good explaining that Mary can take questions, but Fred can't). Having seen many a poor devil caught out by an innocent question they could not answer and many a BOM ruined by an awkward guest, it is not worth the risk!

Instead, in the introduction, ask people who are attending to note down their questions and put them to experienced distributors in the breaks.

Make sure training seminars follow The Steps Of Training

This does not mean that each speaker must follow all the steps of this formula because you may decide that two or even three speakers cover one topic. In this case, what you must ensure is that, between them, the speakers have followed all the Steps, especially the one commonly forgotten: *check they understand.*

Inject the occasional humour, light relief, illustrative story or real-life example

It is not necessary for every speaker to be humorous. Many good training speakers are not. But humour at periodic intervals during the event definitely helps so try to intersperse speakers who are not humorous with those who are.

Whether humorous or not, *any* speaker can tell a story or give a real-life example to illustrate a point. These are essential to keeping an audience's concentration going for longer and for getting a message across in a simple, telling way.

Demonstrate using visual aids

This is part of playing CUPI**D**. Some speakers think that visual aids are crutches for poor speakers. Nonsense. No matter how brilliant the speaker, good visual aids will make them better. It is easier for listeners to understand a topic if it is shown as well as explained. That is why using visual aids is an absolutely vital part of playing CUPI**D**. In fact, if a speaker does not use visual aids, they are not KISSing!

People remember far more of what they see *and* hear than of what they only hear.

Visual aids must be of good quality

You are projecting the image of a high-level business. Tatty visual aids do not support that image.

Good visual aids need not be expensive. The most common presentation tool is the Overhead Projector or OHP. Any computer with a laser or ink-jet printer can produce quality OHP acetates, but be sure to buy the right kind or you might damage the printer. Alternatively, most copy shops can produce acetates from your paper masters at reasonable cost.

You will find your acetates much easier to handle if you mount them on board frames.

Make sure that your visual aids are big enough and clear enough to be seen by people at the back of the venue. For this reason, if you are using OHP acetates, avoid using the dark background colour schemes you will find in many software packages these are in tended for other methods of projection using a much stronger light. To make it stand out, text on any visuals should always be black or in strong colours; therefore avoid pastels.

Always use a clear background for acetates, and white or a light tint for board visuals.

If during your presentation you write on flip-charts or acetates, make sure you write big enough and legibly enough for people at the back of the venue to see.

Choose a good venue

It is not convincing to talk about a high-level business in a cold, seedy bar! If you cannot afford a good location, talk to your own group or leaders from other groups about sharing the cost.

Can everyone see, hear, and be comfortable?

Check out your proposed venue and seating arrangements against this list:

- That those at the back of the room will be able to hear
- That those with hearing difficulties have a seat at the front
- That those with sight difficulties sit where they can best overcome their problem
- That people can see the speaker and the visual aids without craning their necks
- That people can move sideways without digging their neighbours in the ribs. They should also be able to straighten out their legs underneath the seat in front
- That the temperature is right. Over-hot means drowsiness, over-cold means lack of concentration!

- That there will be no intrusive building or maintenance work going on during the event. And that there are no other potential sources of noise, perhaps from passing transport or adjoining rooms. If the venue has windows, you might need to open them during the event; would that let in too much background noise? Some air conditioning is incredibly noisy, so check that, too.

Learn from the organisers of the good events

So often, group leaders start up their own events and then make the same mistakes everyone else has made before! Don't automatically assume that you can improve on another speaker's way of presenting—they could be doing it that way for a reason. If you are not sure why content is included in a seminar, or why it is being presented in a particular way, why not ask the organiser or speaker?

Learn from other people's mistakes: go and talk to them first—and, if you are starting a regular BOM or training, why not ask if they could come and help with the first few? A conscientious trainer will welcome the chance, and out of the shared experience, they might just find ways to improve their own BOMs or trainings.

Make business clothes the required dress code

The correct business dress code varies from country to country, but wherever you are there are bound to be serious business or professional people at the event. Guests may take along a professional adviser. Either way, appearances do count and none of these people are impressed by people they perceive as incorrectly dressed.

At BOMs, you may consider the policy at many well-run meetings of having a distributor at the door who will turn away improperly dressed people. To avoid embarrassment, instruct distributors to make it abundantly clear to their guests what the dress code is.

Start on time

If the meeting starts late, not only does this look unprofessional but those attending may lose some of their enthusiasm.

Is it right that the great majority of keen people, who made sure they arrived on time, are held up for a minority of less keen people who have shown a lack of respect for the organisers and the event?

This is particularly important at BOMs, where guests can get very fidgety if the start is delayed. And it also puts an extra strain on hosts who are trying to keep their guests happy.

Run your events for the many who are ready to start on time, not for the few who are not.

Have a policy on late arrivals

No matter how quietly they enter, late arrivals are a disruption, particularly for an inexperienced speaker. You may consider a policy that any people arriving late are not allowed in; many well-run meetings have a distributor on the door who actually stops late arrivals from entering.

Have a policy on early leavers

Guests at a BOM or new distributors at a training can be disconcerted by seeing people drift off early, no matter what the reason. As meetings often run over time, the people attending should be advised to allow for this.

Leaving early is also an act of discourtesy to speakers and organisers, most of whom are not paid and are giving up their own time. Are they allowed to leave before the meeting finishes?

Many well-run meetings have a policy that, if a person cannot stay until the end, they do not come. They can always attend a later event.

Run your events for the many who arrive on time and stay to the end, not the few who don't

---

Can I remind you of two important maxims:
- That it is the least experienced, least talented, least confident slowest learners who matter most
- That the event is for the benefit of distributors (or their guests), not for the organisers or speakers.

Should you charge for events?

Top distributors can disagree quite strongly over the right policy for charging, and some companies have strict rules on this. My comments assume that your company does gives latitude on this subject. Having said that, different events require a different approach:

Charging for BOMs

There are three forms of BOM.

1. A BOM can consist of a distributor inviting a small group of their own contacts to their own home. Clearly, this is going to be at the host distributor's own cost

2. A BOM can be an upline holding a meeting in their own home or some other venue and asking selected distributors in their group to bring guests. It is only fair that the distributors who attend pay their share of whatever costs are involved; but it would not be normal to expect a profit on the event

3. As a leader, you may decide to encourage your group to hold regular BOMs, weekly if possible, in local venues such as nice hotels. These would be almost always "open" events, to which distributors and their guests from any group can come. Charging for these should do no more than cover costs.

There are four ways to cover the costs of "open" BOMs:

1. Charge a fee to every distributor who attends but guests come free. Alternatively, guests of your group come free, but guests of other groups are paid for

2. Charge a fee for everyone who attends (although a sensible distributor would pay for their own guests!)

3. To get good support, you want as many distributors as possible (whether from your group or others) to make a habit of attending at least one BOM a week (one reason why this is their BACTA target). Having to pay an entrance fee at a time when they may have no money, could militate against that. One solution is that distributors who have reached a certain level on the compensation plan pay a fee, but those who have not yet reached that position come free

4. Distributors below a certain position in your own group come free but all distributors from other groups pay a fee.

If you have speakers or distributors from another group helping you, members of their group should be treated in exactly the same way as yours for charging purposes.

Ask the people who are helping you to run BOMs to keep an eye out for distributors who avoid paying the fee by waiting in the bar while their guests attend the meeting. If one of your distributors does this, ask their upline to have a word with them; if they persist, get their distributorship terminated because they are a terrible example to have in your group. If they belong to another group, take the matter up with their group leader.

Charging for motivational events, i.e., events other than trainings

These are usually bigger, held either as "one-offs" or monthly, quarterly or annually. Unlike BOMs, trainings and other, smaller events, they are not always open to members of other groups.

Some are profit-making ventures, others are not but, provided that the charge is reasonable, it does not seem to make much difference either way to turn-out because people want to be involved anyway.

Charging for trainings

There are three schools of thought about charging for trainings:
- Some say they should be free, to encourage all distributors to attend
- Some say that you should charge only a nominal fee to cover the cost of administration and overheads
- Some say they should be made into profitable ventures for the organisers.

There is an argument that trainings should be free or low-cost to encourage more distributors to attend. My belief is that the extra distributors who might come because it is free or low-cost are those most likely to drop out, and that the more serious distributors will attend anyway. Having said that, you should have an arrangement for those in genuine financial hardship.

Another argument put forward by distributors who complain about the cost of trainings, and by some corporate teams, is that the leaders who run them are investing in the future of their businesses and they are going to recoup this investment by higher earnings and a faster growing group.

That of course is true—but they are missing the point that trainings help just as much to build distributors' own groups as they do the leaders' so, if the argument is that leaders should fund the costs of trainings, then so should the distributors using them.

Leaders give up a lot of time to run and speak at trainings—time which other distributors not so committed are able to spend on their own business-building. Apart from BOMs, the most regular events are weekly trainings for new distributors. These are half- or, more often, full-day affairs and are best run on Saturdays or Sundays, which means that organisers and speakers are giving up their week-ends. Why should they have to subsidise distributors on top of that?

My experience is that those who complain most about the cost of trainings do not themselves help or speak at them. They simply take advantage of what is offered, and if that is all they are doing, it is only right that they should pay for the privilege. Complainers are more likely to drop out anyway, so why subsidise them?

As people in network marketing run their own businesses, there is nothing wrong with the concept of paying for the privilege of learning from the hard-earned experience of the group leaders.

There is also no doubt that people get more out of something if they have to pay for it than if they get it free. Certainly, where trainings are concerned, it is well proven in other fields that people take them a lot more seriously if they have had to pay. Even the Bible says:

> *"People under instruction should always contribute*
> *something to the support of the man who is*
> *instructing them"* (Galatians, 6:6).

Where I can see the difference between a free or low-cost training and one which makes a profit for the leaders is in the quality of the training. There is no doubt that, in general, those which are run with the intention of being profitable are very much better than those which are not. There are some exceptions to this but not many be-cause, although low-cost trainings attract the most altruistic speak-ers, profitable ones attract the best. Distributors therefore only get the best deal from a low-cost training if the most altruistic speakers also happen to be the best—which does not happen often!

So, if you apply the rule that what most benefits the distributors (as opposed to those running an event) is what matters, it is the costlier trainings from which they benefit most! This may seem surprising, but it is borne out by observation.

~ ~ ~

≈CHAPTER 20≈

Have The Best BOMs And Sizzles On The Block

In the last chapter, although we looked at events in general, we touched on BOMs only in so far as they had points in common with other events. In this chapter, we look at the points which particularly affect BOMs. And we will look closely at sizzles.

How important are BOMs?

Not all companies promote the use of BOMs. If they do, the BOM is usually made the central point of the recruiting process. It then becomes a watershed because all prior activity is aimed at getting or "inviting" the guest to attend. After it, if a prospect says 'Yes', the emphasis changes and activity is aimed at getting their new business up and running.

Where BOMs are promoted, they become the public face or the "showcase" of the company; indeed, some companies call them **"showcases"**. Potential new group members are going to judge your business, not on its actual potential in any objective sense, but on what they see of it and how they value what they see. To put it at its simplest:

A guest makes their decision, not on the opportunity itself, but on the sponsor, on the people they meet, on the other distributors they see, and on the BOM itself

---

It is therefore senseless to have BOMs which are anything other than as attractive and professional as possible. This might seem like common sense, but you would be surprised at how many BOMs seem deliberately designed to put off a serious person! Because the great majority are run by distributors, rather than by the company, you will find great variations in the quality of BOMs even within the same company and—unless the group leader exercises control over them—within the same *group* in the company.

For this reason, if you are intending to take a guest to a BOM you have not been to before (perhaps because it is in a different part of the country), it is wise to check it out first either by attending yourself or by getting someone whose judgement you trust to have a look.

How should you structure a BOM?

KISSing applies to your BOM just as to every other part of the business. But $\underline{S}$ also stands for $\underline{S}$hort: 30 to 40 minutes is quite long enough. This is being sold as a simple business. The accent all the way through must be on how simple it is—*anyone* can do it. If the BOM goes on for too long, or if any speaker is allowed to get away from a very simple approach, the BOM will lose some of its effect.

Stick to why guests should do the business (in other words, what might be in it for them), not how they should do it. This is one of the basic rules of recruiting; it is therefore as relevant to the speakers at a BOM as it is to a sponsor. This helps to keep the presentation short and simple.

In particular, keep away from discussing the compensation plan in any detail. Most are extremely complicated and the ramifications are often not fully understood by experienced distributors, never mind new ones! You should, however, explain the self-promotion system, how people choose for themselves where they want to be on the plan, and what they can earn, because these are three big selling points to potential distributors.

The BOM has only two purposes:
1. To give guests enough information to go back to their sponsors for the final discussion to decide whether they should come into the business or not
2. To give guests the reassurances they want about:
    - ✓ The company, its management and its financial status
    - ✓ The product, how it compares in price and quality with its competitors, its saleability and the marketplace
    - ✓ What network marketing is. Some BOMs do not mention network marketing, preferring to promote only a "business opportunity". There is nothing particularly for or against this provided that it is recognised that, at some stage, a new

distributor has got to know and *become proud of the fact* that it is network marketing
✓ The ethics of both the company and the industry
✓ "Can I do it?"
✓ "What support will you give me to do it?"

If any of the content of your BOM does not come under one of these headings, think again about whether it should be included.

Guests have often look at more than one opportunity. While some of these may be dubious and largely sold on "hype"; others, ethical or not, will be hell-bent on *Selling the deal*. It creates a lot of confidence in your integrity, and makes a refreshing change, if you adopt a different approach. First, make it very clear that a guest's decision about whether or not to get involved is a very serious one and the purpose of the meeting is to give them the facts without any pressure, so that they can make the right decision for *themselves*. Second, stress that, in making such a decision, they need to bear three very important points in mind:

- In the longer term, their business cannot be stronger than the product, so they must assess the product
- They cannot be more successful than the company they choose, so they must assess the company
- If they come in, a lot of very busy people will be devoting a lot of valuable time to helping them get their businesses off the ground, so it is important all round that the right decision is made.

This is very far from *Selling the deal*!

Give your group guidelines for BOMs

BOMs are for the benefit of all distributors. You may find some group members quite innocently spoiling it for the others because they do not understand the importance of the occasion. The way to avoid this is to set down some basic guidelines for your group.

To make it easier for you, I have written these guidelines as if you are addressing them to your group, so that you can just copy and issue them:

"1. *Support your BOM.* There is nothing more depressing for speakers than to present an opportunity to a tiny audience! Would you like to take one of your guests to an almost deserted meeting? BOMs are put on for your benefit and the benefit of the distributors in your group, so please support the event and encourage your people to do the same. Guests do not realise that most of the people there are distributors, all they see is a lot of people present and a lively buzz going on.

"Whether you have guests or not, you should go to at least one BOM a week [this is why it is included in the BACTA] because meetings are an important part of team-building. As the rule states: *No one ever succeeded by **not** going to meetings*.

"Distributors owe a responsibility to each other. There is a saying: *If you feel bad, you need the meetings but, if you feel good, the meetings need you*! When you are feeling motivated you should always go along, even if you have no guest to take, so that you can share that feeling with others at the meeting who are feeling "down". Next week, the roles could be reversed and you could be only too pleased to go to a meeting and have someone help you to rebuild your confidence!

"Use meetings to build up a file of distributors who may be useful in the future as **Compatible Distributors** to whom you can introduce guests. Compatible distributors do not have to be in your paylines or even in our group.

"2. *Invite your guest's spouse or life-partner.* Remember that opposition from spouses or life-partners may be a major reason for your contacts not coming into the business or dropping out in the early stages.

"3. *Check with your guest the day before* to make sure they are still coming. Guests who "no show" are one of *The Pigs Around The Corner*. The best way to avoid this is to collect the guest from their home.

"4. *The required dress code is business wear.* Do not be surprised if you or your guest are turned away at the door if you are not wearing business dress, so advise your guests of the dress code.

"5. *Get there early.* You may find the doors locked against you if you arrive late. Advise your guests that this is a business meeting and will start promptly on time.

"6. *Set the scene* [playing <u>C</u>UPID—*<u>C</u>larify the agenda*]. Your guests will feel more relaxed, and will concentrate better on the meeting, if they know what is going to happen. So you should explain beforehand what the procedure will be.

"7.   *Set your guest's mind at rest.* One reason why guests "no show" is because they are frightened of being talked into something or being put under pressure. Make it clear that this is only a presentation and a discussion, and it is not in your interests if people make the wrong decision by coming in.

"8.   *Sit with your guest, not in the bar.* This seems obvious but, to some distributors, it is not! Even if you have no guest, this is not a social night out. Although people should enjoy themselves (this is, after all, one of the great attractions of network marketing), at the end of the day the purpose is to support the meeting, not the bar.

"9.   *Make confidence-building introductions.* Introduce your guest to other distributors to whom your guest may relate [Compatible Distributors]. You can also introduce them to an upline. If another distributor asks you, always be prepared to meet their guest, whether or not they are in your paylines, or even in our group. One day, you may want the same favour in return!

"10. *Hosting.* Although it is obviously better for distributors to host their own guests, in the real world things happen. So you should also be prepared to host guests for other distributors, *whether they are in our group or not*, if the distributor has good reasons why they cannot look after them. Remember, if you are asked to do this, that you may well need the favour returned in the future!

"11. *Poaching is banned!* **Trust** between distributors, even if they are in different groups, is so vital that, if you find any distributor in your group trying to poach, or if one is reported to you by another group leader, act immediately. Not doing so will affect your honest distributors—who, of course, make up the very great majority of your people. Action needs to be seen to be taken.

It can happen that a distributor is asked to host a guest for someone else, at the end of which the guest wants that distributor to be their sponsor. Although it is a bit hard on the guest, the only way to stop abuse of the system is not to allow this.

"12. ***Help guests who are obviously "lost".*** Again, these guests are not fair game for poaching. If the host cannot be found (and it can happen that hosts are unavoidably delayed), you should make sure that the guest is properly looked after. As we saw above, the host does not need to be in our group. Remember, again, that you may well break down on the way to a meeting or be held up in traffic delays, and so need the same favour in return.

"13. ***Help the speakers.*** A speaker cannot be expected to think up new jokes for every BOM and, in any case, the guests will not have heard that speaker before. The speakers are there to help you and your group, so the least you can do is laugh at their jokes!

"14. ***Help the organisers.*** If you have no guest, you should always be prepared to help the organisers in any way you can. The times when this is most appreciated can be in setting up and in packing everything away afterwards.

"15. ***If testimonials are a feature of the BOM,*** you should be prepared to give one if asked.

"16. ***Keep quiet—resist asides.*** Nothing undermines a speaker more than people apparently not listening. You may be telling your guest what a great person the speaker is, but the speaker won't know that and nor will the other guests; if they see you having a whispered conversation, they will think that you are bored.

"17. ***Wear your badge*** [if the company supplies them]. Many distributors feel it is embarrassing or a bit over the top to wear badges, but they serve some very useful functions:

    a) Experienced distributors at meetings are always looking to help other distributors, and badges help to differentiate guests from distributors

    b) Distributors cannot be expected to remember everyone's names

    c) A badge tells an experienced distributor your position on the compensation plan and helps them to "pitch" their conversation in the best way to help you

    d) It looks very good to a guest when a distributor wearing a senior badge saunters over, addresses you by name and apparently knows you well! Little does the guest know that you have never met before—the badges have done it all!

"18. *You and your distributors should be ambassadors for yourselves, our group and the company.* As far as a guest is concerned the BOM is the company's showcase, so make sure it is a good one. BOMs are also often a guest's first experience of the *Network in action,* and we all know how important first impressions are."

[*You can apply many of these guidelines to all events*]

Make your Sizzle Sessions sizzle!

There are a number of considerations which apply specifically to sizzle sessions.

Sizzle sessions are hardly used in some groups and much under-valued in others. Nevertheless, they can be extremely valuable to your business because they are an important way to build Team spirit (part of being a Leaders' AC**T**TER) and they help to keep your business structured and motivated down to a very local level.

A group which holds regular, *properly structured* **sizzle sessions will be very much stronger than the same group without**

Many sizzle sessions over time degenerate into an excuse for a weekly or monthly social get-together for the group. Although this will still have some motivational benefit for the group (anything which gets members of your business together will help the team-building), very little else of business value results from these meet-ings.

One answer is to have an agreed structure for sizzle sessions and then, by Constant Repetition, ensure that your group follows this structure so that everyone is running meetings of value.

Sizzle sessions in groups which have not yet generated their own momentum should be held weekly to begin with, on the same day and at the same time so that distributors can plan around them well ahead.

When a group has generated its own momentum and stabilised, the leaders' sizzles often drop to monthly, although newer groups further down in each leg will still be holding weekly sizzles.

A distributor should attend their upline's sizzle session (this is part of the BACTA). They should also hold a sizzle for their own group. As their group grows, they should then attend sizzles being held by distributors *downline* of them (this target is also included in the BACTA), as part of on-the-job training.

A good way to organise a sizzle

First, a quarter of an hour's formal training

The purpose of the formal training section is to remind your group of the basics. If people are not constantly reminded of the basics, they start complicating the concept and wander off track. The only way keep on the On-Track Path is by Constant Repetition, and sizzles are a perfect platform for this. You can take a chapter from one of the books in *The Secrets Series* or The STARS Leadership Programme as a base for your presentation.

This fifteen minutes of formal training is also an excellent way for your potential speakers to get used to the idea of public speaking and formal training. But fifteen minutes is quite enough; the purpose of a sizzle is not to hold a formal training session.

Second, the notice board

You should pass on communications from the company, your uplines and, of course, anything you wish to communicate to your group.

Make sure you *Check for understanding* (one of the Steps of Training)—in other words, that everyone is clear on what those communications mean.

Third, the rest of the session as Reactive Training

This means that the meeting should react to what the group members need rather than to what you want. Sizzles are primarily Reactive Training meetings (page 125).

So both the formal training and the notice board should be despatched as quickly as possible. Then you should throw the meeting open to whatever topics those attending wish to discuss. *It is vital that you keep your own wishes out of the equation at this stage,* which means that the leaders who run the best sizzles are those who keep their own egos furthest out of sight!

However, as leader, you should keep everyone to the point under discussion. Also, make sure that quieter people are encouraged to speak and to raise topics for discussion, and that the more assertive ones do not dominate the discussion and do not dictate the choice of topics.

When someone asks me to look into why they are finding it difficult to get people to attend their sizzles, the reason is often that the leader is "hogging" the limelight or that they are impatient of people's views. The fact is that people want and need to be heard and treated sympathetically and with respect. If the meetings do not allow them to clear the air and deal with the problems that are causing them concern, it is hardly surprising if they stop attending.

How to control the quality of the sizzles in your group

If you are working with an inexperienced distributor who has developed a big enough group to start their own sizzles, you will need to give them some help until they are confident of running them on their own.

Several days prior to the event, discuss with them what formal training would be most valuable for the first fifteen minutes of their sizzle session and then ask *them* to prepare the notes for the presentation. This way, they will learn far more than if you do it for them. You should then discuss their notes with them to make sure that the content is right.

The formal training should be backed up by visuals. Most fifteen-minute sessions will only need one, but some may need two or three depending on the topic. As sizzle sessions by definition should be confined to small groups, an A3 sheet for the visual is normally enough. The alternative is to give each distributor photocopied A4 sheets. Either way, group members should take away notes to read at home, as part of Constant Repetition, and to pass onto their distributors who did not come to the sizzle.

Go as a guest to as many downline sizzle sessions as you can. Although the sizzle leader and his or her group will find it great motivation to have you there and that in itself is a great reason for going, *your purpose is not to take the meeting over.*

The reasons for attending sizzle sessions are partly to keep your profile high and partly to work with your sizzle leaders on the job, helping them to present themselves better (being a better Leaders' ACTTER), to present their content better (KISSing and playing CUPID) or to help their people get more out of the sizzle sessions. Agree in advance who will do what, and review the sizzle afterwards with the leader.

In particular, remember to **R**espect your sizzle leader's sphere of influence (page 108—part of being a Leaders' ACTTE**R**). You do this partly by making sure you do not take the meeting over. Confirm their position in the minds of their group as much as you can, and thank them in public for having invited you to their meeting. That way, you will build their loyalty and confidence in you, and you will always find yourself welcome at their meetings.

~   ~   ~

≈CHAPTER 21≈

How To Keep Your Group Singing From The Same Hymn Sheet

**Winning Leadership =
Training + DIRECTION + Motivation**

Even if you only want a small group, you don't want distributors who all go charging off in different directions. If you want a large group, it becomes absolutely vital that this doesn't happen. But how do you create the sense of a team playing together, rather than a bunch of individuals doing their own thing? There is only one way:

Direction means having leaders in place capable of duplicating your philosophies, methods and standards throughout your business

---

To do this, therefore, you as a leader need to:

Spot the leaders!

If you want to be a big business builder, a different **Keystone Law** will give you a better idea of what you need to do: *How successful you are will depend on how many active teachers and leaders you develop in your group.*

Given that anyone can become a leader and teacher, let's not over-state what a leader and teacher is. Remembering that *Doing the job is teaching it; teaching the job is doing it*:

Anyone who will stick to doing the job as it should be done and will teach others to do the same is a leader and teacher

---

That does not sound as if you are asking for much and you are not, so you might expect that leaders would be easy to find. But this is one of *The Pigs Around The Corner* because, as the City of Dreams story tells you (Chapter 6, *Get Off To A Winning Start*), although all can make the effort, few will.

Your other problem is, just as you cannot prejudge where distributors are concerned, *nor can you prejudge who will or who will not succeed as a leader*. There is only one way to leaders, and that is by continuing to recruit new members to the group. Recruit enough, and eventually the winning leaders will start to emerge.

What do you look for in a leader?

The same as you want in a distributor (page 62) only more of it:

- **Do they have a *burning* desire to succeed in network marketing?**
- **Do they have an *insatiable Hunger to Learn***
- **Will they *consistently apply* what you teach with *Focus* and a *Bulldozer Mentality*?**

People with these qualities bypass the need for talent; the more of these qualities they have, the greater the leaders they will become. But they are very hard to find, which is why we call them "Stars". So don't make the mistake of passing them over in favour of other group members who may initially appear to have more obvious leadership qualities.

So, when you are looking for leaders, focus on these three qualities above all else. Just because we are talking about leaders does not mean that you are looking for intelligence, previous experience, education, articulateness or the "right" background any more than you would with a distributor. Sticking to this principle may mean having to spend a lot of extra time teaching someone because they seem to have absolutely nothing going for them except a Burning Desire, a Hunger to Learn and a determination to apply what they learn, but:

Would you rather work for six months carving a solid rock into shape for your business, or would you prefer to put less time and effort into moulding putty?

How long should you spend with a trainee leader?

Remember: *Although attitudes determine how well they **will** act, knowledge determines how well they **can** act.* Therefore:

A trainee leader should not be left to get on with it on their own until they are at least as good as you are at teaching and leading their own business

---

If they are not, standards of teaching and leadership will dilute as they cascade down your group.

Many groups stop growing once they reach a certain size, suffering from Sponsoring Sieve disease. You will often find that the cause of this is that the leaders at the top of the group and those in their immediate sphere of responsibility do the job right but, because they do not have the right leadership training in place, this has gradually diluted as the message has gone down the network.

But if you teach your leaders properly they may well end up better than you because you will have taught them everything you know, to which they will graft all their own talents and abilities. Then you truly will enjoy the fruits of your efforts!

Some trainee leaders will have your brains and experience picked clean in a matter of weeks. Others may take six months—it does not matter because *There is no time-limit on creating winning leaders.* Provided they are on the On-Track Path, stick with them for however long it takes. It is hard enough finding people with a Bulldozer Mentality without giving up on them because they are slow learners!

How to find and develop "Stars"

People who are prepared to put the effort in to be active leaders ("top dogs" and "first lieutenants", pages 20 and 21) are very rare. So when you spot one, arrange with their sponsor to make them your protégé: someone whose training you will make your special responsibility. Their sponsor will be delighted because they will earn from that distributor for doing nothing, and it also releases them to work with someone else.

Now include them in every meeting and activity you can. Make them your shadows. If they are not present at an activity, involve them in the planning and review it with them afterwards to pick out the lessons.

When you have finished teaching your first "Star", you should move on to find another while your first "Star" teaches *their* first. This gives you four "Stars" in your business. The four "Stars" will each then teach a new one, giving you eight "Stars" in your business.

You can make the Geometric Progression work on your "Star" leadership base just as you can on your distributor base. If it takes an average of four months to train each "Star", at the end of two years you will have 64 in your business. Even if it takes six months, you will still have 16 "Stars" in your business—with 32 just six months later. In the real world, this may happen much more slowly because you may not be able to find enough people prepared to make the necessary commitment. But I think you can see the point I am making: you need a system to spot the "Stars", to make them as good as they can be, and to ensure that they do the same with their "Stars". Sadly, most people squander the potential of their "Stars" by assuming they have nothing to teach them and leaving them to their own devices.

While your group will grow well without "Stars" (which is what this Programme is about), each one who does come in will generate explosive expansion for your business. If you use the system I recommend to find and develop them, "Stars" will increasingly begin to appear in your business, but it will take time. So, in developing leaders, you will need the *Patience to give the Geometric Progression time to work* (Patience is one of the Six Winning Attitudes).

Direction means Communication

Unless your group is kept fully up to-date with all developments and with everything they need to know, they *cannot* do the best possible job for you.

Company internet sites or communications such as newsletters or emails that go out direct to each distributor, are rarely a complete answer. If you want to ensure that your group is kept fully briefed on activities within the group, you must take on this responsibility for yourself.

By reporting on developments and success stories within your group, your own newsletter helps to foster **T**eam spirit (part of being a Leaders' AC**T**TER). By promoting trainings and quality learning materials, it can help foster a Hunger to Learn. And, by using Constant Repetition to drive home the basics of doing the business, it can help ensure that your group stays on the On-Track Path.

The phone is an excellent way of getting communication through to every distributor. Any good upline is always looking for excuses to phone their group, and having information to pass on is a good one!

You can also use the "notice-board" section at sizzle sessions to get communications out to all your group.

Emails and internet sites, while sounding the attractive and easy option, are less effective than the phone because you cannot beat the interplay of live communication.

Direction means that each distributor has a sense of purpose

If people do not know what their destination is, how do they know in which direction to go? They don't—so they stop. A sense of direction is created when people have heart's desires to aim for. If they know what those are, they can be shown in which direction to go.

People forget their direction in life very easily *unless someone keeps reminding them*. It is up to you, a winning leader, to make sure that the need for focusing on their purposes is *continuously* stressed throughout your group as an essential part of achieving success. This is why *Focus on your purpose* and *Focus your actions on success* are included in the Six Winning Attitudes. And, as we saw, your main tools for achieving this are the ATAC Lifeplan, the Heart's Desires Card and the Planning for Success form, which define the destinations, and the BACTA, which draws up the plan for reaching those destinations.

Direction means having a standardised training system throughout your business

This is the main benefit for you of *The Secrets Series* and The STARS Leadership Programme. If everyone is being taught in the same way, everyone benefits. Perhaps more than anything else, this creates a strong sense of everyone in your group "pulling in the same direction".

Direction means giving a good example

Being a winning leader means doing everything you did to become a successful network marketeer and a winning teacher—*but doing more of it—and showing other people how to do it!*

More than in any other business I know, in network marketing, people take their lead from the top

---

Give a good example to your group and you will be giving the strongest possible direction to your leaders and to your people.

The pace of the pack is determined by the pace of the leader

Never forget that you were once a struggling distributor. So one excellent example is to give a helping hand to anyone who asks for it, whether they are in your business or not. If you generously give of your time, knowledge and experience to other people, you will not be a just winning leader, you will be a great leader!

Each night, review the day by asking yourself, *If every one of my group does what I did today, how would my business grow?* Did you really behave like someone leading from the front? Did you really give your group a good example not just in what they did see, but in what they didn't see? In other words, are you practising what you preach as a habit, whether people are there or not? Because, if you do not, why should they?

Direction means controlling the ethical standards of your group

This was covered in Chapter 14 of *Get Off To A Winning Start*, including a useful Code Of Professional Ethics. Only you, as the leader, can ensure that everyone in your business sticks to the standards you lay down.

Direction means controlling the structure of your business

One reason why large incomes are available through network marketing is because there is no theoretical limit to the number of front-line people you can develop directly beneath you—unlike conventional organisations, where it is generally accepted that one person can *properly* manage only between five and ten people reporting directly to them.

The reason why one person can successfully manage an open-ended number of people frontline is because the techniques required to be a winning recruiter, retailer, teacher, leader and business-builder are so simple that they can be quickly and easily learnt and taught—*provided the teacher and leader go about it in the right way.* Once a frontliner has an established business, they can safely be left to get on with it; although if you are wise you will keep an eye on them to make sure they stay On Track.

The next question is: how do you decide whether to recruit a new frontline or whether to work with leaders and group members in existing legs of your business?

Control the structure by "anchoring" each leg

Each person you take on frontline is creating a new leg for you. And each leg is in fact a separate business in its own right. You can compare this with a conventional businessperson who owns many different "companies".

Your next aim is to **Anchor** or **Establish** that leg. Anchoring or establishing means developing it to the stage when it no longer needs your day-to-day input because the distributors are perfectly capable of "growing" that leg with no help from you.

The strategy we talk about here may need to be adapted to make best use of the compensation plan of your company.

There are three basic rules to building a solid business:

1. Anchor each leg before moving onto the next one……

2. …… by building deep before building wide

3. Teach your group to do the same.

When you start a new leg, you are what is called **The Momentum Generator** in that leg. If you move onto a new leg before it is fully anchored, you are taking the momentum generator out and that leg may well collapse, which means that you have wasted all the time and effort you expended on it. In that case, all you are doing by re-cruiting frontline is to make up for the legs that are collapsing, in-stead of recruiting to expand your business. You have allowed your group to contract **Sponsoring Sieve Disease.**

To avoid this and at the same time structure your business properly, adopt the business strategy of *Working deep, not wide* (Chapter 6, *The Secrets of Group Structuring*). In practical terms, building deep means, first, limit how many frontlines you start with. You cannot start with too few but you can easily have too many. Second, then do not recruit anyone else frontline until at least one of your previ-ous frontline legs is anchored.

How many frontlines you should start with depends on, first, how much time you are devoting to the business and, second, how much time any frontliner you are working with is giving to the business. If you are *part*-time but you recruit a *full*-time frontliner, you owe it both to them and to yourself to keep your frontline to one until their business is up and running.

If you are working all hours and the first few people you recruit are part-time, you could start with as many as five or six but, if you have any doubts at all, err on the side of taking on too few.

Therefore building wide simply means that you are starting new legs while existing ones are not anchored.

How can you judge when a leg is anchored?

The two most common approaches, neither of which I recommend, are:

1. You leave a leg and move on as soon as you have a "serious" distributor somewhere in that leg capable of showing the business.

    Apart from distributors who bring in everyone frontline to themselves and therefore have no strategy at all, this strategy is by far the most frequently used but it has two serious flaws:

    a) What happens if that one "serious" distributor drops out? The leg will collapse

b) Even if that one serious distributor does not drop out, you will have moved to a new leg before they know as much as you about the business.

If you pass the leadership baton for a leg to a distributor who cannot do the job as well as you can, according to the Theory of Duplication they will do the same, so the quality of tuition and leadership will fall at each level. But if you teach each momentum generator not to pass the hands-on responsibility for a leg until they, too, have found a momentum generator and taught them to teach and lead *at least as well as they can*, your standards of tuition and leadership will continue right to the bottom level of each leg.

2. You have anchored the leg once you have "taught 'A' to teach 'B' to recruit 'C'", as explained by Don Failla in his book *The Basics*[2].

The philosophy I would recommend is a third one:

A leg is only anchored when:
1. You have found a **Momentum Generator** in that leg and taught them to teach and lead at least as well as you can, *and*
2. The leg is generating its own momentum.

In other words, you should create new momentum generators in that leg *before* leaving it not, as is generally the case in the industry, uplines hoping that momentum generators will appear *after* they have stopped working in a leg.

Business-building in this way can sound like a drawn-out operation, but it is an illusion caused by impatience and lack of experience that, by building wide (or leaving legs too early), you will build a bigger business more quickly. Once again, the lesson is to be patient and to work methodically. Particularly if you use *The Distributor's Action Plan*, the All-Out Rocket Action Programme in Chapter 22 of this book or the fast recruiting methods in Chapter 14 of *Breakthrough Recruiting & Retailing*, you will create a solid base to your business more quickly and, once you have done that, business ex-

---
[2]Published by MLM International

pansion will be both dramatically faster and more solid than with groups where the leaders have tried to cut corners.

Don't be fooled by a Fool's Paradise

In deciding whether a leg is anchored, you need to allow for drop-out rates. These vary enormously, but the average seems to be between 70% and 90% per year in a group of any size. On this basis, of the first ten distributors in any one leg, only one or two will stay. Hardly a strong leg! Therefore, even if you have an apparently strong leader emerging in that first ten, it might still be too soon to start a new leg.

Yet ten names on a computer print-out looks good and will allow a new distributor into the Fool's Paradise of thinking that their business is growing well and that they can move on to recruit a new frontliner.

In some compensation plans, one of the benefits of a promotion is that you qualify for royalty payment on an extra generation. For instance, you may start by receiving royalty on three generations but, when you reach a certain position on the compensation plan, your royalties may then be paid on four generations.

This is excellent news, provided that you actually have four generations to be paid on! People who have structured their businesses wide rather than deep may find that, when payment on that extra generation "switches in", they have not built a business deep enough to take advantage of it, whereas someone who has built their business deep in the way we have described, may well find themselves benefiting immediately from payments on the extra generation.

In the example we have just given, you could therefore say that a leg is anchored when you can be sure of four generations of qualifiers in at least one line of the leg—in other words, four serious distributors downline of each other—so that you can take immediate advantage of the benefits of promotion. This may not sound very important until you realise that each level in your business potentially *has more distributors on it than **all** the levels above **added together!*** (Chapter 4, *The Secrets of Successful Group Structuring*) Looked at in this way, it is not inconceivable that your income will double overnight each time you qualify for an extra generation for payment.

So another definition of an anchored leg is:

1. You have found and taught a network marketeer in the leg who can teach and lead *at least as well as you can,* and
2. In at least one line in that leg, you are taking advantage of all your generations for payment.

There is a final big benefit to building deep, and that is that your personal recruiting will get easier and easier.

One of the most compelling recruiting aids is that you have helped a downline build a successful business, giving yourself and others the confidence that you can help someone else do the same

---

This will make your Get-Active phone calls much more effective:

> *'Fred—you don't know Mary, but she has only been with me for three months, and she already has a group of 30 people! Join me, and I can help you do the same thing.'*

This means of course that you have got to create a success story first, and the very fastest way to do that is to concentrate on one leg.

I once met a distributor who, through an astonishing recruiting effort, brought in 280 people frontline. Three months later, only two legs remained active; one month later, he was down to one! Although this is an extreme instance, you will find many less dramatic examples of the folly of building wide rather than deep.

Now, to round off The STARS Leadership Programme, we turn to the problem of how you, as a winning leader, can motivate your group to do what it takes to succeed.

~ ~ ~

≈CHAPTER 22≈

The All-Out Rocket Action Programme —The Fast Way To Build A Solid Business

(You should read this in conjunction with *The Distributor's Action Plan* and Chapter 14 of *Breakthrough Recruiting & Retailing*)

This is called **The All-Out Rocket Action Programme** because it is the ultimate in Rocket Action. No matter what your destination is, this is by far the fastest way to get there. It does this by overcoming the first of the leaders' and teachers' "Pigs": *Getting people to make Get-Active phone calls!*

It is a very exciting plan because massive, concentrated effort is applied to everyone's Contact List as soon as they sign up. It is a very exciting plan because people see results in days rather than weeks, or weeks rather than months. It is a very exciting plan because everyone is either accompanying someone else or being accompanied by someone else, everyone working in partnership, no one working on their own, and that is much more motivating than people struggling on in isolation.

It is also the fastest way to build a business because it telescopes work—a programme that would take most distributors weeks or months is concentrated into a few days. And it is by far the fastest way to generate **Momentum** in your group.

It is also the most solid way to build a business because it is by far the best way to overcome people's worries about whether they are "good" enough to do the job. Even the least charismatic and talented of people will build a strong group more quickly by using this technique.

Despite all its advantages, it is best to warn you in advance that only a small proportion of your people will be prepared to do what the Rocket Action Programme demands. However, don't let that worry you because that will be enough to put you on a fortune. And once two or three set an example of what can be done, you will find it increasingly easy to sell the idea to the others!

How does the All-Out Rocket Action Programme work?

There are certain issues that stand squarely between you, as a group leader, and the success that you want. I outlined these in *The Distributor's Action Plan* but they are worth repeating:

The Six Points of Reality

1. That unless distributors have quick recruiting success, they will drop out
2. That the majority of distributors will not do what they need to do to achieve what they want
3. That the *whole* of your success is based on how many Get-Active phone calls are made in your group
4. That unless they are accompanied by an upline, the vast majority of distributors do very few phone calls
5. That unless people are accompanied in everything they do, you will lose all the untalented distributors and many talented ones too, which will make a big dent in your pay cheque
6. That without *URGENCY IN ACTION!* in your group, you will not make the money you want as fast as you can.

The better you as a group leader solve The Six Points of Reality, the faster and the bigger your group will grow

The All-Out Rocket Action Programme is the only real solution to The Six Points of Reality. That, together with making sure that people are accompanied in everything they do, is based on the concept that people will make *many times more* phone calls with someone else than on their own. And this means that your business will grow *many times faster!*

How the All-Out Rocket Programme works

Week 1

1. Starting on Monday, because this is psychologically a good day, attack your own Contact List, making 10 to 20 calls a day. If at all possible, find an upline to help you; but if you can't, don't delay: get the calls done! The sooner you start and the more calls you make, the quicker your business will take off! Book to see anyone interested as soon as possible.

2. When you have recruited the first person who will:
   (a) give you a Contact List of *at least* 100 names and
   (b) agree to join the Rocket Action Programme and work with you intensively over the next week, stop your warm market phone calls. Let's call this new distributor, "Mary".

   You may find Mary on Monday or Tuesday, after just 10 or 20 calls. However, if you are unlucky, you may need all 100 calls to find her. That does not matter because if you work with her properly, your business is going to take off anyway whether you find her sooner or later.

   Many people will not agree to 2(a) and (b) above, so *please note that you may have to recruit several people before finding your Mary*.

3. Sit down with Mary and diary in as much time as possible to work together in the following week.

4. When you find Mary, don't cancel the rest of your 2-2-2 appointments. They have been booked and out of courtesy they must be seen; and you can use them to start training Mary in 2-2-2s.

5. If anyone from these appointments wants to join the Rocket Action Programme you may have a problem freeing up the time to work with them intensively. First, see if someone upline or cross-line can help. If that doesn't work, there may be another new distributor you can put them together with (again, even cross-line). This is what we call **The Buddy Method:** two new people working together. If you can't do that, you can **Stack** them under Mary or another suitable downline. Of course, you should only stack under distributors who are in the Rocket Action Programme. Stacking is an emotive subject: some people

are for, some very much against (Chapter 14, *Breakthrough Recruiting & Retailing*).

Week 2

6. On Monday, start making phone calls with Mary on her Contact List. Because you must give Mary a good example and you are also in a leadership relationship with her, you really should be able to make 20 phone calls a day, especially bearing in mind that Mary will increasingly do more of the calls herself as her confidence increases.
7. Stop further phone calls on Mary's behalf when the two of you have found *two* distributors off Mary's list who agree to 2(a) and (b) above. If you have stacked someone under Mary from your Contact List (see step 5 above) you will only have to find one person off her Contact List.

Week 3

8. Following the guidelines in *The Distributor's Action Plan*, you now introduce the **Monday Night-Phoning Night system** to your group. On Monday, you take one of Mary's new distributors and Mary takes the other, both of you doing exactly the same as you have just done with Mary.

Week 4 onwards

9. Keep repeating the process, working further down Mary's leg of your business, and making sure everyone else is doing the same.
10. Bring together everyone who is working the Rocket Action Programme for regular sizzle sessions (Chapter 20). With all this action going on, this is the best way to meet and support your most dynamic new people.
11. Don't leave Mary's leg until it is properly anchored (Chapter 21). But, as each leg gets anchored, start the process again with a new leg.

You will need to be flexible with the timings

Although I have given an example of a three week plan, in practice, there is a lot of luck involved:

1. You cannot always book the 2-2-2s to be seen that week. Some may hang over to next week or even later
2. Luck dictates how many people on any given Contact List happen to need the business now, and will therefore sign up
3. Not everyone either wants to, or can, start the Rocket Action Programme straight away.

But the principle behind the All-Out Rocket Action Programme still holds true even if it takes weeks or months longer than my example, because you will still have taken months, even years, off the speed at which your group builds. Even if you do not find two people for a new distributor in their first week, you will find them very much more quickly using this method than in any other way.

Note how, by building a commitment to the All-Out Rocket Action Programme in your group, you are automatically building habits of *Urgency in Action*, and you are also making sure that people being accompanied in everything they do becomes the culture of your group.

But be warned that even if a new distributor fast-tracks their business with the Rocket Action Programme, the initial excitement may not be sustained, and they can quite easily drop out of the Get-Active phoning sessions. The first flush of their enthusiasm coupled with your own *Urgency in Action* will get most people through their early days, but longer lasting results will demand a Bulldozer Mentality.

The Peter Bloomfield telephone system

Peter Bloomfield is one of the top British group leaders. His system addresses two major industry problems: the first is our old one of getting people to make Get-Active phone calls. The second is getting contact lists.

The Peter Bloomfield system is similar to that in *The Distributor's Action Plan* and the All-Out Rocket Action Programme, and you should run it in the same way, but with one major exception:

Distributors *never* phone their own contacts

A distributor's contacts are always phoned by an upline. Or looked at the other way round, a distributor never phones their own contacts, only those of downlines. This has big advantages:

1. It makes irrelevant what is probably a distributor's biggest fear: having to phone people. In Get-Active phoning sessions, *all* the calls are made for them

2. It makes it much easier to get a distributor to agree to someone making the calls with them when it is explained that: *"I don't want you to touch the phone—I'll be doing it all for you. All you have to do is sit and listen"*

3. It takes advantage of the fact that, generally speaking, distributors much prefer phoning contacts for other people than on their own account. The great majority are happier with a system that means they never have to contact their own people

4. Under this system, an upline takes on board the full responsibility for building a downliner's business, which is the finest way to apply the Keystone Law

5. Recruitment actually goes up! Except when a distributor is one of those rare people who has great credibility with their contacts, the number of 2-2-2s booked in each phoning session actually increases.

However, absolutely key to the conversion rate going up is the Get-Active phone call, which differs slightly but in very crucial ways to the standard one. First, the usual *"Fred and I are building a business together and Fred has suggested that you might be just the sort of person......"* changes to *"I've been chatting to Fred. He speaks highly of you. I'm expanding a business in your area......"* The first makes Fred's credibility an issue (so you should still use it if Fred is one of those rare people with great credibility), the second does not.

The next stage is that the usual *"Would you be interested"* becomes *"...... And I wondered if you would be averse to looking"* or, alternatively, *"Are you open to looking"*. Most standard openings have the drawback of creating a barrier in the contact's mind which hopefully can be overcome by either the skill or the credibility of the person making the call, or the contact's own interest in the product or need to find another source of income. The openings in the Peter Bloomfield system have no such drawback. In fact, they make it very easy for a contact to agree to have a look.

You can also see that this is a much more relaxed approach which, first, more distributors would be comfortable with and, second, is a much less threatening approach for contacts, making it even easier for them to say "Yes".

It should be stressed that the Peter Bloomfield system is **not** the same as the one where distributors pass over their contact lists to uplines who happen to be strong on the phone. That has been tried time without number and it never works because there is no downline duplication going on. The Peter Bloomfield system should only used in the presence of the downline whose list is being worked, because you want to teach and encourage them, too, to use the system with their downlines. Otherwise you will not get multi-plication of effort (Chapter 9, *The Secrets of Successful Group Structuring*) going on.

The second problem addressed is the one of getting contact lists. Even in the various methods in *The Distributor's Action Plan* and The STARS Leadership Programme, it is best to aim for a Contact List with at least 100 names (the only exception is "Big Al" Tom Schreiter's Stair Step Solution, but that requires more recruiting skill). In the Peter Bloomfield system, because an upline is making all the calls and generally gets better results, it is usually sufficient to ask for only 20 names for the first Get-Active session.

Once a distributor has seen how well it works, they are usually very willing to supply all the names the upline asks for.

Turbocharging the All-Out Rocket Action Programme

There are two ways you can do this. I have given you the example of working with only one person a week, something even a part-timer can easily do. But you could work with several—although the more you work with, the more careful your planning needs to be. Even if you don't think you could sustain this long-term, you can set yourself a short-term target of working with, for example, three people a week for, say, your first six weeks. I think you can see the explosive effect this will have on your business.

Full-timers, of course, should be able to work with around five or six people a week.

A good way to turbocharge the phone call part of the Rocket Action Programme is to get access to two phone lines. If you can afford it, you could have a second line installed at your home—or you may already have one for a fax machine or internet access. Given that most distributors should be able to make their own calls after an hour or two of working together, with two lines you can:

- Make calls on their behalf on one line, while they make calls on the other, or
- Work with an inexperienced distributor on one line while a more experienced person uses the other, or
- Have two distributors making calls, while you alternate between them, giving them feedback and taking some calls for each in turn to give them a break.

Once you build up experience with this approach, you can even work with a third line and three distributors. Imagine the excitement and momentum that this could generate in your business!

Some groups have local distributors' clubs with facilities for communal Get-Active phoning, and some distributors have offices where they offer this facility. All these systems recognise that distributors will make many more phone calls when they are surrounded by other people than when they are on their own.

What about people who refuse 2(a) or (b)?

Many distributors write off people who will not do a proper Contact List or who will not work with them to phone their people. But, if you keep in touch in the right way, some will join the All-Out Rocket Action Programme later with the added bonus that they have found out the hard way how not to do it! In the meantime:

1. Try to get them to commit to a BACTA (Chapter 16) and phone them daily as outlined on page 99
2. If you cannot get a BACTA, phone twice a week just to ask how they are getting on: I recommend Wednesday, because it is nicely mid-week, and Friday, because it is seen as the end of the week.

Remember, don't put any pressure on them—just ask them if there is any way in which you can help. If they are finding the going difficult (and they usually are!), an offer from you to make some phone calls with them "just to see what the problem is" or "just to get things going" might be accepted with a sigh of relief! Keep contacting them regularly until they either convert to the All-Out Rocket Action Programme or become inactive.

What if you have blown your warm market?

If, by the time you read this, you have been working for a while as a distributor, you may not have a big enough Contact List left to work this system. So pull your leaders together and train them to bring new distributors in on the All-Out Rocket Action Programme. Then work with distributors in each of your leader's legs in turn, helping them to get the Rocket Action Programme going.

The Rocket Action Programme makes recruiting easier!

All the activity generated by the Rocket Action Programme creates excitement and momentum in your business, and this makes recruiting easier for everyone.

> **How much more powerful is it when you can say to a contact: 'Look at the business I have just built with one of my people. Would you like me to do the same for you?'**

~ ~ ~

≈CHAPTER 23≈

It's Easy To Be A Great Motivator!

Winning Leadership =
Training + Direction + MOTIVATION

We have looked closely at training and direction; now we will look at how to be a successful motivator.

This is, perhaps, the aspect of leadership that worries people most. They think that a great motivator must be a larger than life character with a powerful, magnetic personality and lots of charisma. They think that they must be able to get up on stage and raise the hearts and minds of people with gifted oratory. And they think they have none of these gifts. The odds are that you, reading this, are probably right—you probably do have none of these gifts! *But that does not mean you cannot become a winning motivator, able to build a large, successful business.*

If you are not a larger than life character, you can replace this with Conviction (part of being a Leaders' ACTTER) in what you are doing and an ability to communicate that to your group.

These are things anyone can do. It depends only on how much they want to and what action they are prepared to take to make it happen. By the time you finish this chapter, you should feel comfortable that there is nothing here you could not do.

What is motivation?

Motivation is a concept rarely understood by conventional managers. They see it as something they impose on other people, and it is often defined as the "carrot and the stick" principle. Carrots are pay rises, promotions, the trappings of status and a whole variety of incentive schemes, competitions and bonuses. Sticks are fear of losing one's job, missing pay rises and promotions, being shown up in front of one's work-mates or incurring the wrath of superiors.

You can see that there is a lot of bribery and fear-mongering in this. But none of this is real motivation. Real, ongoing motivation consists of four things:

1. People *wanting* to work for their boss and their company, not *having* to
2. People working for what *they* want, not for what the company wants out of them
3. People knowing what their heart's desires are
4. People seeing how they can achieve those heart's desires through working in your business.

What conventional business calls motivation is short-term in its effect and depends mainly on either offering material gain or status, or threatening their loss. These are hardly noble appeals to the emotions! In short, motivation is based on company values.

The motivation we are talking about is based on *people* values: people working because they want to work for a particular individual and people working for what they want to achieve for themselves, not for what the company wants out of them. If people work for you because they want to, that is long-term motivation. If people see how they can achieve their purposes through working in your business, that, too, is long-term motivation.

Let me just rephrase what I said above, because it is so important:

Long-term motivation means motivation from *within* the person being led (*self*-motivation), not motivation imposed from outside by the leader

---

I will show you how to truly motivate your group long-term.

Loyalty is a great motivator

Loyalty is not a right, it is an *earned* privilege. Traditional managers would have you believe that, because they are senior to you, they are entitled to expect your loyalty and because a company or organisation pays you a salary or wage, it has the right to "buy" your loyalty.

Employees, too, either individually or through their trade unions, now believe that they have rights to income and employment without the responsibility of giving value back to their employer. This, of course, at least in part, stems from the example they have received from their employers.

In a healthy environment, a company or organisation should expect that it must earn your loyalty by respecting and treating you properly—then, of course, it is entitled to it.

In a healthy environment, managers know that they are entitled to an employee's loyalty only if they take steps to earn it—then, of course, they are entitled to expect it. That way, managers know that they must work very hard at being good managers of people.

In a healthy environment, employees know that they are entitled to the loyalty of their company and managers only in return for quality work and good productivity—then, of course, they are entitled to it.

I have gone into this in some detail because you will find many people who come into your business expecting support from you (in other words, your loyalty) but doing only the minimum in return. They expect you to build their businesses for them. They expect you to run training sessions for the group at week-ends but they can have the week-end off. They expect you to host a guest at a BOM or do a 1-2-1 for them (they don't believe in 2-2-2s) because they want to socialise. They feel that a dinner invitation is a good enough reason to miss your regular Tuesday evening sizzle. In other words, they feel they have rights without responsibilities.

You will also find group leaders who feel that their position entitles them to the loyalty of their group without them having done anything to earn it.

Loyalty is a two-way contract

As a winning leader, you must expect that you are only entitled to loyalty if you earn it. The more you do that, the more loyalty you will earn and the more loyalty you can expect in return.

The only true, worthwhile loyalty a distributor can give you is to repay your efforts on their behalf by their efforts on your behalf

---

...... such efforts, of course, being just as much to their own benefit!

Of course, on day one, a new distributor has not yet had a chance to do anything to earn your loyalty. So, in the first instance, they deserve *all* your loyalty as of right.

But thereafter, you are looking for as much loyalty back in terms of them doing the tasks they agree to do, to the best of their ability.

Whether they do their tasks well or badly does not matter, it is the actions and the attitude behind them that matter: did they do what they agreed, and did they do it as well as they could?

If the answer is "No", leave that distributor to their own devices because they no longer merit your loyalty. If you continue to work with them, you are not only making them **Dependent** on you, but you are also giving a bad example that will, according to the Theory of Duplication, spread throughout your group. So find instead another new distributor to work with, or give your loyalty to those group members who are repaying your loyalty with their own.

Earn loyalty by learning to love your people!

Love is the great motivator. Think of the people in your life who matter most to you; it could be your parents, your spouse or loved one, your children. It could be brothers or sisters. Of all these people, you can say publicly that you "love" them. But we also love many other people in our lives: great friends, close colleagues, caring teachers, spiritual leaders, a mentor who has guided us, faithful employees or (if we are lucky!) a "boss" who really helped us.

These are the people in your life for whom you will do the most. For some, you would be prepared to give your life. What has motivated you to show such loyalty to them? Love. If other people can generate that motivation in you through love, you can use the same power to motivate others.

To be a power, love must be shown. If it is not, it might as well not exist; it has no value. If you want to make it mean most to the recipient, show it in the way the recipient most wants it to be shown. In the case of your group, they value your love most in the way you **appreciate** them, show **pride** in them, **praise** them, **care** for them and for what you **do** for them.

Show **Appreciation** for what people do for you and they will work harder, more willingly and more happily for you.

Show **Pride** in your group and it will feel pride in itself, and a group that does that is a very strong group! Pride is a massive motivating power and one of the Six Winning Attitudes.

Giving **Praise** shows both love and appreciation. Look for opportunities to appreciate individual efforts and praise them. When you have to criticise, balance this with appreciation for the effort they are making on your behalf and praise for what they do well.

At meetings or in newsletters, pick out people to compliment. But not just the obvious high-flyers; the vast majority of your group will be part-timers, often looking only for a small income from network marketing. They, too, deserve to be appreciated. It is not motivating for them if the only individuals you ever choose for mention are the high-flyers. If you use incentive schemes, make sure that part-timers and small business-builders can also win something.

Show you **Care** about your people, and care about them you should because you will get nowhere without their efforts! Even in a business of thousands of people, each one is a special person in their own right.

One drop of rain achieves nothing, but enough drops of rain will cause a mighty flood. One distributor may earn you little, but enough of them will make your ATAC Lifeplan come true!

Go to as many meetings as possible, circulate among your group and have a few encouraging words with as many people as possible, because this shows how much you care.

Distributors in any group split into two: those with established (or anchored) businesses and those without established businesses. Group members with established businesses can get into the comfort zone of spending too much time with each other but it is not each other you need—you are already successful people. You can only keep your success going by continuously applying the Keystone Law and making *new* people successful—in other words, by continuously helping other distributors to get their businesses established. So you should spend *as little time as possible* with each other and *as much time as possible* with group members who have not yet managed to get their businesses established.

At trainings, meetings, business or social events, those with established businesses should make a point of not sitting or grouping together, but of being well spread among those who do not yet have established businesses. The only exception might be speakers at a formal training; they are often best seated at the back, leaving the front rows for those who matter—the trainees. If you are used to conventional business, mixing with other ranks might not be the way you were taught to behave as a manager, but in our business, it pays to show your people that you care enough to seek them out and want to spend time with them.

If you make sure your people feel the better for you passing by, and if you teach your leaders to do the same, then you truly care for your people and they will care for you

---

Leaders in traditional business and institutions are appallingly bad at making people feel appreciated for their efforts and praised for their good work; and when did you last hear of a manager in conventional business who really cared for their people or was proud of them? Yet:

Nothing else earns as much loyalty. Nothing else so easily turns a winning leader into a great leader.

Working hard for your group earns its loyalty

If people can see that you will "pull out all the stops" for them, the good ones among them will do the same for you. Working with them on the job, making them aware that yours is an ever-open door, an ever-ready phone, an ever-listening ear and that nothing is too much trouble, are all ways of showing that you will work hard for them.

But, as I have said many times, you should not work harder for them than they are prepared to work for themselves. There is a fine dividing line here but an important one because, *once people become Dependent on you, they will no longer be loyal to you;* they will simply take you for granted and expect you to do things for them.

Too many leaders have found out to their cost that you can do too much for people *who are not doing enough for themselves*

To your amazement, these people will not be there for you when you need them.

Making people realise that their success matters to you, earns their loyalty

This is another way of applying the Keystone Law. You should be more concerned about the success of your people than you are about your own: **A**ccountability in being a Leaders' **A**CTTER actually works. If the group feels that you are helping them for themselves, you will build loyalty. If they believe that you are only helping them to help yourself, their loyalty to you will be limited by their own self-interest; in other words, they will be using you in the same way as you are using them. It sounds like a contradiction, but it is true:

If you care more about other people's success than about your own, you will actually be *more* successful—and happier

---

Would you rather look back on life and congratulate yourself on how successful you have been, or would you rather look back and congratulate yourself on how many other people have become successful through your efforts?

People are most loyal to their Mentor!

The role of mentors has become very undervalued, partly because of the breakdown of the family unit (mentors were often elders of the family), partly because we no longer respect the wisdom of our elders, and partly because value is no longer placed on practical experience.

Yet outside immediate family and love relationships, people still give their greatest loyalty to a mentor. If it is the mentors who generate the strongest feelings of loyalty, does it not make sense for *you* to become the mentor of your group?

You may be confused as to the difference between a mentor and similar roles played by teachers and leaders.

The dictionary defines a mentor as, "A wise or trusted adviser or guide". The Leaders' ACT<u>T</u>ER shows you exactly how to become <u>T</u>rusted by your group, and a good teacher and leader does become an adviser or guide in *business* terms.

But a mentor goes further than that. A mentor becomes a "wise and trusted adviser or guide" in *all* aspects of a person's life, whether business or private.

In the final analysis, a teacher or leader is there for the business; a mentor is there for the distributor

---

Network marketing, more than almost any other business, has very blurred dividing lines between business and private life—in fact, the two soon become inseparably linked. This is caused partly by the nature of the business which is person-to-person in the home, partly by how the family, whether they are officially signed up or not, get involved in a distributor's job, and partly because there is not the separation of time between business and personal life which you get in most jobs.

A distributor's quality of work is also directly affected, especially in the case of a new distributor, by the quality of their private life in a way which happens in few other occupations. This gives a mentor an important part to play in the health of a group.

And we are also in a people business (which is why *People buy People* is one of the Six Winning Attitudes), so in the long run you will prosper by putting your people's interests before your own short-term concerns. Becoming a mentor, because of the way it deepens and cements relationships, turns a winning leader into a great leader.

So how do you become a mentor?

- Accept that you cannot make anyone choose you as their mentor; the choice rests entirely with them, not with you. They will only do so when:

  i) They trust both you and your judgement, and

  ii) They realise that you will put them and their interests before those of you and your business.

- This sounds like a lengthy process: in fact, if you approach people right, you can have them voluntarily coming to you for advice within minutes of meeting you. The process of helping people to find their purposes, involving as it does very intimate discussions of a person's innermost feelings and desires, also gives you a chance to create a mentoring relationship very quickly

- You must, quite genuinely, give them the right advice even if it is not in the immediate interests of you or your business. Once you recognise that the trust this creates between you and your people will add dramatically to your business interests overall, even if in the occasional individual case it does not, this becomes easy to do

- In order to avoid a situation of Dependency, only choose to help those who are making best efforts to help themselves, and make it clear that this is their side of the bargain. This may sound hard but, in fact, you will be doing the best thing for them. If you let people become Dependent on you, you will do them more harm than good. The finest gift you can give anyone is to teach them how to stand on their own two feet and learn how to meet life on their terms

- Become a wise person, able to give wise advice. Wisdom is no longer a respected attribute, yet it is vital to being a good mentor. There is no mystique to being wise. Anyone who follows these guidelines will be a wise person:

  ✓ Listen hard and *fully understand* what the problem is and how the person really feels about it (not how they ought to feel) *before* giving any advice

  ✓ Give advice not from the standpoint of what you believe, but from the standpoint of what that person needs

✓ You do this by keeping yourself out of the equation, ignoring your beliefs and attitudes and taking on their beliefs and attitudes

✓ Be non-judgmental. Show pride in your protégé

✓ Give respect to everyone and everything, especially to those who think differently to you, no matter how strong your views on that matter

✓ Accept that is sheer arrogance to assume that your views must be right and that all others who think differently are wrong

✓ Listen and *learn* from others. Truly wise people have humility in that they know everyone, no matter how young, naive or inexperienced, can teach them something. *Every situation is a learning situation if you let it be so*

✓ Keep the emotions out of a discussion so that the real cause of a problem can be found and the best answer sought

✓ Make time for those people who need your time.

Becoming a mentor is one of the most rewarding things in life. It sets up a very special relationship that transcends normal business relationships. But it imposes on you a responsibility to advise at all times in the interests of those you are advising.

The best form of motivation: SELF-motivation

We saw earlier the four forms of self-motivation. We have covered the first of these: how to make people want to work for you. Now let's look at how you can apply other three.

Working for what they want, not for what you want out of them

If people are working for what they want, not for what you want out of them, they are with you because they want to be, not because they need to be—obviously a much more self-motivating position to be in!

It is very easy to do this: all the way through I have been saying, *Don't dump your expectations onto your people*—in other words, *Let them decide their aspirations for themselves.*

Help people to find out what their heart's desires are

It is all very well letting people choose their own aspirations for their businesses, but it only works if people have aspirations of their own to put there! Too often, people have become rudderless through years of following the aspirations of others, mainly bosses, parents or life-partners. When these are removed, they no longer have their own to put in place. Look at what can happen to parents when their children leave home, or to people when they retire.

Employed people can become so used to responding to employers ruling their working lives that they find it very difficult when they have to replace that with self-imposed disciplines. The reason is the same—they have not yet got clear in their own minds the purposes worth working for.

Few people are self-motivated, because the things they truly want for themselves have disappeared under a mountain of unwanted "baggage" which they have steadily accumulated throughout their lives. Self-motivation starts to come alive, and is only possible, when a distributor learns to throw away all that unwanted baggage and to focus on only those things they truly want for themselves.

This is why we place so much emphasis on teaching people to define their purposes in life.

The best way you, as a winning leader, can apply the Keystone Law is to help your people find *crystal-clear* heart's desires that really *excite* them

---

Then, show them how to do the job right.

But your job does not stop there. It may seem illogical that people should forget about the things they really want for themselves, but they do! That unwanted baggage, given half a chance, soon starts to accumulate again! So you should constantly remind your group to use their ATAC Lifeplan and Heart's Desires Card, and *Focus on their purposes*.

Show your group how they can achieve their heart's desires through working in your business

We have established that once a distributor believes an action is a "must", they will do it.

If people believe that working in your business is the way to their heart's desires, how much will you have to motivate them?

It is no good to you that people know what they want to achieve in life, unless they believe that they can achieve these *through your business*. The Focus Equals Outcome Ladder (page 78) shows you exactly how this process works. The Planning for Success form is so powerful because it makes the direct connection between a distributor's purposes and your business.

You therefore have to give your group the confidence that network marketing, your company, your product and, most important of all, *your leadership* are the right vehicle for their ambitions: Both making yourself **A**ccountable for and your **C**onviction in their success— being a Leaders' **AC**TTER—help here.

Motivate by getting rid of *de*motivation

Doubts, worries, fears and lack of belief are the biggest barriers to success, and to motivation. There is not room in a person for both motivation and doubt. A person cannot reach their highest levels of motivation until all their doubts have gone. Even a small doubt can significantly affect a person's ability to succeed.

Like a small branch that falls into a river, a doubt or fear soon start to collect other debris around it, having an ever-increasing effect on the free-flow of the water

---

The worst thing you can do as a winning leader is to add to those worries! That does not mean that you should bury your head in the sand. If a problem is there, it is there. But contrast these ways in which two leaders dealt with the same problem:

- One came in with a long face and said, 'We have a problem. I want you all to see if you can find an answer to it'

- The other came in with a jaunty air and said, 'I think we have a temporary hiccup here! I want each of you to come up with ways round it and then we'll discuss who has the best solution.'

The first focused the group on the problem, the second on the solution. Accept any problem as being only a temporary deviation and, in public, always show complete confidence in success. If you do not, why should your group?

Share your worries only with your mentor (yes, you too should have one!), with trusted downline leaders whom you know will react positively to the situation and with uplines whose judgement you trust. Apart from that, keep your worries where they belong, shut away in your private office.

Personal development—the greatest weapon at your disposal

At the heart of the Eight Must-do Activities is by far the most important of them: the Winning Attitudes. This is where personal development comes in.

As well as believing in you, your people need to believe in *themselves*. They know that other people can succeed in your business, but can *they*? Personal development teaches them, first, that they can become dream-creators, that they can achieve, and, second, how to change their attitudes to achieve their heart's desires.

The greatest means you have at your disposal to make yourself as successful as you can be is undoubtedly the power of your mind. The greatest instrument at your disposal to make your business as successful as it can be is undoubtedly the collective power of the minds of your group.

Look again at the Focus Equals Outcome Ladder on page 78, and you will see that of the four steps, *three are all in the mind*. In the Pyramid to Success (page 41), of the five levels, *four are in the mind—and at least half the fifth!*

No longer do sportspeople think that they can reach the top of their sport without the practise of personal development. They accept that attitude is more important to winning than natural ability or the amount of training done—important though those are.

Yet those of us from conventional organisations so often dismiss personal development as something a bit New Age, perhaps showing a weakness of moral fibre. In conventional business, if you practise it, you certainly do not admit it!

You cannot retain that belief in network marketing. Indeed, it is often called "*the* personal development business" because the one thing that really matters is having the right attitudes. Nearly all the winning leaders in our industry are great champions and promoters of personal development. Very often, this is because they became dream-creators came through practising it. So you may have attitudes which do not require the practise of personal development to succeed but, I promise you, most of your group will not. However, you can show them how to acquire them.

So, to become a winning leader in network marketing, you have to:

- Become an expert on personal development (which is not difficult)
- Make it part of your group's culture of training and leadership
- Constantly encourage your group to use it.

Personal development is a big subject, needing a book to itself in The STARS Leadership Programme, *Network Marketeers… Supercharge Yourself!* Or there is my generic book called *How To Achieve Everything You've Ever Wanted*. If you have taken my advice, you will have already studied and be benefiting from these and other good books, tapes, CDs and videos on the subject.

~ ~ ~

≈CONCLUSION≈

If you put into practise everything we have talked about and lead by example with passion and conviction, I promise you that, whether you consider yourself a natural leader or not, you *WILL* build a highly motivated network of leaders and a group that will be positively *buzzing*! You, too, can join that elite band of great network marketeers at the top of this fine profession, the one profession which is truly there for all.

I hope that the wonderful business of network marketing may be the way to making your ATAC Lifeplan come true and open the way to the lifestyle you have chosen. And may you, as a winning teacher and a leader, have the enormous satisfaction of helping many others to make their ATAC Lifeplans come true.

> *"Give me your determination, give me your action,*
> *give me your willingness to learn, and I will show*
> *you the way".*

Give to your people the commitment which I gave to you at the start of this book, and you will be a winning teacher. Give to your group this same commitment, and you will be a winning leader. But more than that:

Keep giving value, keep making people feel the better for you passing by, and you will be a winning human being

---

Than that, there is no finer accolade.

> *And may your God or good fortune go with you in*
> *your endeavours in life.*

~ ~ ~

≈GLOSSARY≈
Terms Used In The STARS Leadership Programme

(Any term in *italics* is defined elsewhere in this Glossary)

Accompanying people in everything they do. On-the-job (as opposed to *Arm's Length*) training. Probably the most important concept in network marketing, which is why it is included in the *On-Track Path* and the *Six Points of Reality*.

ACTTER and Leaders' ACTTER. How to present yourself either as a distributor or as a teacher or leader, depending on the circumstances:

- **A**ccountability. Be responsible for helping contacts or customers make the right decision for themselves; be responsible for showing and helping group members to make their *ATAC Lifeplans* a reality
- **C**onviction—how you must always appear to potential new distributors, your group, and customers
- **T**ell, not Sell when presenting to potential distributors and customers. For teachers and leaders, this becomes **T**eam-mindedness: make all your people feel part of your team
- **T**ruth = Trust
- **E**njoyment
- **R**espect.

All-Out Rocket Action Programme. The ultimate business-building strategy and the ultimate in *Accompanying someone in everything they do*.

Arm's Length Training. Telling distributors what to do, rather than showing them on the job (see *Accompanying people in everything they do*). There are two forms of Arm's Length Training: *Formal Training* and *Reactive Training*.

ATAC Lifeplan. **A**bundant **T**ime, **A**bundant **C**ash. **A**bundant **T**ime to be the person you want to be, do the things you want to do and have the things you want to have, and **A**bundant **C**ash to fund those aims. Each person's ideal lifestyle. The ATAC Lifeplan is so-called because you can only make it a reality by ATTACK-ing the things in life that get in the way of it.

BACTA. See *Business Activity Agreement*.

Balloon Business. A large business built on poor foundations, in contrast to a *Cannonball Business*, which is a large, solid business.

BOM. See *Business Opportunity Meeting*.

Breakaway Group. In many networks, distributors' groups "breakaway" from their upline groups once they reach a certain position on the compensation plan. This does not mean that they become *"Top Dogs"*, unless, of course, they want to. Most do not, continuing to co-operate with their uplines on trainings, BOMs, events and day-to-day running.

Bulldozer Mentality. One of the *Six Winning Attitudes*. Keeping going despite every obstacle. The Bulldozer Mentality is expressed by Urgency in Action.

Business Activity Agreement (or BACTA). An agreement made by a distributor with themselves to carry out all those activities which history has proved are essential to success.

Business Opportunity Meeting (or BOM). Also called Showcase, Business Presentation, Briefing and other names. A regular, ideally weekly, presentation of the business by experienced distributors for the guests of other distributors.

Cannonball Business. A large, solidly built business, in contrast to a *Balloon Business*, which is a large business built on poor foundations.

Catherine wheel Action. Action not leading to one's purposes (cf. *Rocket Action*).

Chicken List. The people to whom a distributor is embarrassed or frightened to show the business. Everyone has a Chicken List. Because they are, by definition, those to whom the distributor is closest to or most in awe of, they are the "hottest" part of anyone's Contact List.

Compatible Distributor. Someone to whom a prospect might relate because they have something in common, such as the same background, occupation, ethnic group, age or sex, or have had to overcome the same problem.

Compression, The Principle Of. When distributors are paid on *Generations* as opposed to levels. Each generation (which may consist of many levels) is compressed into one level for the purposes of royalty payments.

Constant Repetition. This is essential to ensure that group members, leaders and teachers stay on the *On-Track Path*, and avoid complicating the business. It is also essential for teaching slow learners and people who lack business experience, and for replacing bad habits with good ones.

CUPID. How to *KISS*:
- **C**larify the agenda
- **U**nfold at their speed. Unfold in bite-sized chunks. Unfold one topic at a time
- **P**resent logically
- **I**llustrate the achievability
- **D**emonstrate with visual aids.

Dependency. A distributor has learnt to depend on you to build their business for them, or that they are prepared to work only when you are actually with them.

Figure-of-Eight Attitude. You are the focal point of the figure "8". Above are your uplines, below are your downlines. You are the point of communication both ways.

"First Lieutenants". People who want to be part of the decision-making process of the group, but do not want to run it (compare with *"Top Dog"*). Akin to a director in conventional business who wants to be a member of the board but does not want to run the company. Often big business-builders in their own right.

Focus Equals Outcome Ladder. A ladder to success showing how heart's desires both start and finish the process.

Formal Trainings. *Arm's Length Trainings* which follow an agenda set by the trainer(s), as opposed to *Reactive Trainings*.

Generation. Payment by levels would give uplines little royalty income, due to the 70% to 90% inactive rate of a group in any given month. To solve this, companies calculate based on qualifiers, i.e. active distributors who have turned over more than a pre-set monthly qualification figure (see also *Compression*).

GUIDE Sequence. The Steps of the Recruiting Process:

> **G**et-Active Step
> **U**nfolding Step
> **I**nvestigation Step
> **D**ecision Step
> **E**nsuing Step.

Heart's Desires Card. An inspiring summary of the ambitions that matter most to you, and you aim to achieve through your business. To be referred to as often as possible, feeling that you have achieved them already, and to keep yourself focused on your purposes.

Keystone Law. Where distributors are concerned, this states that *Your path to success lies ONLY through the success of your people.* Where big business builders are concerned, it is: *How successful you become will depend on how many trained leaders and teachers you develop in your group.*

KISS. **K**eep **I**t **S**tirringly **S**imple. How to present the business and training. To KISS, you play *CUPID*.

Learning LAWR. The sources of knowledge: **L**isten to successful distributors, **L**isten to tapes and CDs, **A**ttend meetings and Trainings, **W**atch videos and **R**ead books on your opportunity, network marketing and personal development.

"Lone Wolf". A distributor who insists on "doing their own thing", usually refusing to co-operate with uplines.

Momentum Generator. A distributor applying the principles of motivation.

(Eight) Must-do Activities. The essential activities in The STARS Leadership Programme: **S**upport events, **T**each, **T**arget, **A**ttitudes, **R**ecruit, **R**etail and **S**tructure your group. They are in turn driven by the *Keystone Law*.

On-Track Path. Putting in the time promised *and* willing to be *Accompanied in everything they do and* willing to apply what they have learnt with the right attitudes, particularly having Focus and a *Bulldozer Mentality*.

Pigs Around The Corner. Problems faced by *all* new distributors, who should therefore be warned about them. Teachers and leaders have their own *Pigs*.

(Six) Planning Commitments. The commitments you should seek from any distributor before agreeing to work with them:
1. Commitment to what they want from the business
2. Commitment to learning
3. Commitment to putting what they learn into practice
4.   Commitment to doing a proper Contact List
5. Commitment to your teaching strategy
6.   Commitment to their Business Activity Agreement.

(Six) Points of Reality. The issues to which every distributor has to find solutions, as a leader of their group, before they can become successful.

(STARS) Pyramid to Success. The stages of achievement through which every successful person in any field of human endeavour has to go. A useful trouble-shooting tool to isolate where problems in a person's performance might lie.

Reactive Trainings. *Arm's Length Trainings* which react to the group's needs, as opposed to *Formal Trainings*.

Rocket Action. Action not leading to one's purposes (cf. *Catherine wheel Action*).

Showcase. See *Business Opportunity Meeting.*

Sizzle Sessions. Small, regular meetings designed to help and motivate the group. The topics should, by and large, be chosen by the group, not the sizzle leader.

Sponsoring Sieve. The point at which new group members being "poured in" at the top of the "sieve" only balance those falling out as inactive at the bottom of the sieve; thus the group has effectively stopped growing.

Stacking. Generally, a sponsor puts new distributors into their own frontline. They may, however, "stack" them in a downline distributor's frontline. The downline distributor would then become the official sponsor.

"Star". One of the rare breed of charismatic, natural leaders. It is estimated that only about one in two thousand distributors fall into this category. The purpose of The STARS Leadership Programme is to show the other 1,999 people how to succeed as big business-builders.

(STARS) Steps Of Training. The steps that should be taken when training:
Explain:
▪ What to do
▪ Why do it and
▪ Why do it that way.
Show:
▪ How to do it.
Check:
▪ Check they understand (i.e. test absorption)
▪ Then check that it is working (i.e. check effectiveness).

Teacher's Profile of Success. Knowledge and understanding of their subject➲ is a Leaders' *ACTTER, KISSes* and *Plays CUPID*➲ follows the *Steps of Training*➲ uses *Constant Repetition*➲ all of which lead to Good Habits of Work.

Thirty-Minutes-A-Day Habit. Thirty minutes a day spent studying tapes, CDs, books and videos. Fifteen minutes on recapping and fifteen minutes on new study.

"Top Dog". A top leader who runs their own group autonomously, akin to a managing director in conventional business (compare with *"First Lieutenants"*).

(Six) Winning Attitudes. One of the *Eight Must-do Activities* which drives the other seven. The Six Winning Attitudes are: Have Pride; Have A Bulldozer Mentality; Have Focus; Be Patient; Be Hungry To Learn; People Buy People.

From The Network Marketing Academy on network marketing

> If you want to see how David Barber can help you explode your business, see him at **www.davidbarberinternational.com**

The Secrets Series. **The starter series of The Network Marketing Academy, the finest series in the world for new distributors:**
- Just What Is… Network Marketing?
- The Distributor's Action Plan
- The Secrets Of Successful Recruiters
- The Secrets Of Successful Teachers & Leaders
- The Secrets Of Successful Group Structuring.

The STARS Leadership Programme. The advanced series of The Network Marketing Academy and the finest series in the world for serious distributors and leaders:
- Get Off To A Winning Start In Network Marketing
- Breakthrough Sponsoring & Retailing
- How To Lead A Winning Group
- Network Marketeers… Target Success!
- Network Marketeers… Supercharge Yourself!

Other titles
- Network Marketing: A Different Way Of Doing Business
- How To Give The Best Parties On The Block!

David Barber's *Living With♥Heart* **Personal Development Programme**
- How To Achieve Everything You've Ever Wanted
- Adam & Eve Your Way To Love And Happiness.

Group discounts
Are you a group leader? If so, we can supply you with books to sell to your people at exceptional discounts. For full details, contact the publishers:

The Network Marketing Academy, 7, Braddons Cliffe, Braddons Hill Road East, Torquay, Devon TQ1 1HR.
Phone/fax 01803 296733.